Pacific Northwest Travel Guide & Stories

Explore Washington's Evergreen Forests, Drive the Scenic Route Through Oregon's Quaint Beach Towns, and Hike Through Idaho's Stunning State Parks

RuthAnn Cole

Edited by Romy Hoffman

Access a Free Printable Resource

.... showcasing the "Unusual, the Uncommon, and Unique places to Explore" in the Pacific Northwest!

Simply visit: bit.ly/3oNrOg

... to discover this FREE access to a collection of **Peculiar Adventure Locations**!

Be sure to check it out at: bit.ly/3oNrOg
or scan the QR code below:

Table of Contents

PACIFIC NORTHWEST

Introduction

There's something magical about the Pacific Northwest, where forests are thick, the mountains are tall, and the beaches are rugged." – Unknown.

The Pacific Northwest offers stunning natural scenery, revitalizing rainy weather, an invigorating coffee culture and diverse, active outdoor lifestyles.

This area has been known to cover multiple areas including parts of Canada, and northern California. This book will focus on the northwestern part of the United States, comprising of Washington, Oregon, and Idaho.

This region offers mother nature in all her glory from snowy mountain peaks, leafy forests, golden deserts, and raging rivers to monolithic shorelines. Where else can you experience deserts and forests in the same state?

If you love the sea, you will find a very diverse coastline with oddities like the Devil's Punchbowl with its unique geology and Cape Disappointment, where many lives were lost on the ragged coastline. A worthwhile stop on your journey is Deception Pass in Washington, where ancient forests meet the ocean. Seaside, Oregon is a popular destination with bird watchers and photographers looking for the ultimate scenic shot. Idaho's Lake Cascade and Priest Lake offer pristine beaches with perfect temperatures. You will find some of the most picturesque camping sites and best inns in the region.

Wherever you go, you will find beautiful spots and welcoming little towns with the best seafood. Local restaurants pride themselves on using only the freshest, locally sourced produce of the highest standards. Even the most avid foodies will find it hard to fault the exquisite meals served in even the smallest establishments. If you are a wine connoisseur, you will find something for your palette in the Willamette Valley. If you prefer beer, you will enjoy the craft beers produced in Eastern Washington which arguably can compete with the best craft beers internationally.

If culture or art is more your scene, you will find a few hidden gems in the smaller towns. Seattle, Portland, and Boise offer symphonies, operas, dance, and drama. Visit one of the many art galleries, some of which have art by Native Americans on display.

For the more adventurous travelers, dive into the deepest lake in the United States at Crater Lake National Park. Go whitewater rafting on the Rogue River, explore the underground world of the Lava River Cave in Oregon, or go rock climbing near the Priest Lake area. The possibilities are endless.

Interested yet...? If so, you may feel overwhelmed by all the information available. Most of us travel on a budget and you may find it difficult to plan your trip. Some good news: We will help you find all the hidden gems the area offers in order to plan the adventure of a lifetime! This book will be your guide, giving you the benefit of the author's more than 35 years of living and traveling in the Pacific Northwest area.

Jim Belushi is a well-known comedian and actor. His life was featured in a show called "Building Belushi," where he carefully fixed up old barns and other buildings on his property before constructing his timber-framed dream house next to the river. Although the actor was born and bred in Chicago, he lost his heart to the picturesque Rogue River in Oregon.

Another celebrity "rocker/actress/writer," Carrie Brownstein, was born in Seattle and moved to Olympia, Washington, during the nineties. Here, she found a lively music scene. She founded the band Sleater-Kinney, which was called "the best group in America" in its time (Marcus, 2001). She fell in love with Portland and created the sketch comedy series Portlandia, which parodies life in Portland, Oregon. It first aired in January 2011 and had a run of eight seasons. This Northwest girl made it to the big time!

Another musician who made Portland her home is Canadian-born singer K.D. Lang. She told audiences in Portland for many years that she wanted to move to Rose City before finally doing so in 2012. In 2014, she played a caricature of herself in Carrie Brownstein's Portlandia. Portland was quick to claim her as "our own" (Campuzano, 2018).

One of the most well-known female politicians in the United States was born in Sand Point, Idaho. Sarah Palin was governor of Alaska and ran for vice president in 2008. She got her degree in communications from the University of Idaho in Moscow before getting her first job as a sports reporter in Anchorage, Alaska.

Well-known author Ernest Hemingway lived in Sun Valley, Idaho while writing his famous novel For Whom the Bell Tolls in 1939. He fell in love with the area and bought a house in Ketchum, where he lived until his death in 1961. The house is now listed on the National Register of Historic Places and is known as the "Ernest and Mary Hemingway House."

Want to find out more? Let's start exploring?

Chapter 1: The Pacific Northwest

The Pacific Northwest is one of the few places in the world where you can see five major volcanoes (Mount Rainier, Mount St. Helens, Mount Hood, Mount Adams, and Mount Baker) from a single vantage point.

(https://www.nps.gov/places/sunrise-point-south-exhibit-panel.htm)

An Overview of the Pacific Northwest

This Pacific Northwest boasts of a wealth of natural wonders. The Olympic National Park in Washington is a vast wilderness area featuring rugged coastline, glacier-capped peaks, and ancient forests. The Cascade Range, which runs from Washington to northern California, is home to stunning mountain scenery, and a wide range of outdoor activities, from skiing to hiking and mountain biking.

The Pacific Northwest also boasts a rich cultural heritage, with strong indigenous traditions and a thriving arts community. The region is home to many museums and cultural institutions, including the Museum of Pop Culture, the Seattle Art Museum, and the Portland Art Museum. Idaho boasts of its Western and Native American heritages and preserves and honors the importance of each.

Finally, the Pacific Northwest is known for its innovative tech industry, with companies like Microsoft and Amazon headquartered in the region. This has led to a thriving startup culture and a dynamic economy that attracts entrepreneurs from all over the world.

In short, the Pacific Northwest offers something for everyone, from outdoor enthusiasts to culture vultures to techies. Its stunning natural beauty, vibrant cities, and rich cultural offerings make it a truly unique unforgettable destination.

The Pacific Northwest's climate leans towards cool temperatures and cloudy skies specifically between the ocean, and mountain ranges and forests, while semi-arid climates are found to the east. The region boasts hundreds of miles of old-growth forests. Some of the oldest trees are hundreds of years old and reach nearly 300 feet in height. If you are lucky, you may even see the northern spotted owl, which is an endangered species native to the area.

You will revel in the beauty of majestic mountain peaks, and you will be spoiled for choice. Mountain ranges in the region include:

- Coast Mountains
- Cascades Range
- Blue Mountains
- Olympic Mountain Range

The Coastal Range runs parallel to the coastline, and although it is not the highest of the ranges, it offers some steep cliffs with spectacular views over the sea. The Blue Mountain ranges (locally called "the Blues") are found in central Oregon, over the Snake River along the border with Idaho, all the way to southeastern Washington. They were given the name "Blue Mountains" due to the blue hue from their pine and fir lined ridges. There are many protected areas in the Cascade Range, which include several national parks, forests, and monuments. People who want to climb the Himalayas or the Andes often train in these mountains first. There are also some highly rated ski resorts with trails suitable for both novice and advanced skiers.

What is the Pacific Northwest?

Officially, the Pacific Northwest is made up of northern California, Oregon, Washington, Idaho, and the southern part of British Columbia. The climate for most of the region is cool and wet, which explains why old-growth forests with some of the biggest trees on earth are found here! Many trees in the Pacific Northwest are believed to be older than 1,000 years; some of them are the giants of the plant kingdom. The spectacular mountain ranges split the region in two. The east side is warmer and drier and the western side next to the coast being cooler with high rainfall. The best time to visit is in the summer months between May and October. This is when temperatures and rainfall are moderate.

States Located in the Pacific Northwest

When Sharon, a great friend from high school, came home for a visit, we just had to take a road trip and ended up visiting all three states of Washington, Oregon, and Idaho!

Our journey started in Portland, Oregon. This vibrant city is known for its friendly people, interesting boutiques, and bohemian downtown. Our other friend Jody, a fitness fanatic, just had to find somewhere for her morning jog. She roused us, far too early in the morning, to accompany her. We had some smokey rich coffee bought from a friendly lady in a food truck, while Jody got her exercise. Mount Hood's snow-capped peaks offered us some background scenery while the sun rose to another glorious summer day.

The drive from Portland to Boise, Idaho took around six hours. Admittedly, we took our time as we had to stop in Pendleton, LaGrande, and Baker City for various bathroom and drink breaks along the way. The landscape changed as we drove; we were now on farmland with weathered barns and huge silos. We stayed in the quaint Franklin

House, a renovated "icehouse" dating back to the 1890s. The next day we ventured into the greenbelt on bicycles. Jody, of course, was the leader of the pack, with the rest of us huffing and puffing behind. If it wasn't for the ice cream truck we found halfway, we would not have made it back.

Our next stop was in the Emerald City of Seattle, Washington. Famous for being the home of Starbucks, Seattle offers more than just good coffee! A visit to the Olympic National Park is definitely worth it or do as we did and take a leisurely drive along the coastline to delight in the stunning natural beauty of the area.

The next day we took the "road less traveled" and caught a ferry to the San Juan Islands, just off the Washington coast. Here it seems as if time stood still and we spent the day on Orcas Island (the largest island of the group) hiking in the forests and next to the sea; we were even lucky enough to spot a pod of orcas, after which the island was named.

What Makes the Pacific Northwest Special?

There aren't many places in the US that have as many different kinds of landscapes as the Pacific Northwest. Most visitors know about the rugged beaches, longstanding forests with their giant trees, and snow-capped mountains. Few know about the wildlife, fields of flowers, and quaint little towns that somehow remind them of Europe.

Part of the unique allure of the region is the stark contrast of rainforests close to desert regions.

Mount Hood, Oregon

This is perfectly illustrated by Steens Mountain, Oregon, which can have snow right through the year. At the foot of the mountain lies the Alvord Desert, which is a salt pan with less than seven inches of rain per year, making it one of the driest spots on the continent. During the dry years, many sand-sailing enthusiasts race across the pans on their version of ice boats—not for the faint of heart!

Even though there are a lot of fast-food places in the area, the real heart of Pacific Northwest cuisine is local seasonal food that can please even the pickiest eaters. "From farm or boat to table" is a concept that has been perfected by the many chefs who love to cook with food from the area, turning it into delicious and unique dishes.

James Beard, one of America's best-known food writers, grew up in Portland. He fondly remembers his childhood, gathering wild huckleberries, eating crab and clams fresh from the sea. After a visit to a well-known restaurant in Grays Harbor, he mused that he had never eaten more delicious seafood anywhere in the United States.

Another food celebrity of the region is chef Matt Dillon, who farms and produces blackberries, beans, onions, carrots, potatoes, and pimentos. This entrepreneurial chef also breeds free-range chickens, ducks, goats, pigs, sheep, and Highland cows, many of whom end up on his renowned menu. Matt believes that the ingredients should be of such high quality that they speak for themselves and don't need more than basic seasoning.

 *Don't Laugh, I Followed the Sheep...*

Arriving in Ketchum, Idaho, at the beginning of October on my way to hike in the Cascade mountains, I was surprised to step out of my hotel on Main Street and into the Big Sheep Parade. You guessed it, I was officially part of the parade and surrounded by 1,500 woolly sheep. As I could not get out of the throng, I followed... like a sheep, and I experienced one of the high points of my travels by ending up as part of the Trailing of the Sheep Festival celebrating the Basque culture in Idaho.

I was treated to sheep shearing, dancers from different cultures, and, of course, many culinary events. I attended lamb tastings, lamb cooking classes, and even a farm-to-table lamb dinner. After buying several wooly items from a very interesting lady who could not tell me enough about the Panama sheep she farms, I got invited to visit her farm the next day, where I had an encounter with a ram that ended up with me being covered in Idaho mud!

The night was filled with listening to the many stories told by ranchers that could double as storytellers while having a sumptuous dinner at the Pioneer Saloon on Main Street. Now my time in Ketchum was at an end, and I was on my way to meet my hiking partners in Mount Rainier National Park. I am so thankful to have walked into the Trailing of the Sheep Festival, as it turned out to be one of the highlights of my trip!

Whether you like big-city life or prefer small towns, the region has something for you with its vibrant cities, charming towns, and friendly people. If you are a night owl, you may be surprised to find an abundance of trendy nightlife to enjoy.

With natural produce aplenty, healthy living is second nature in the Pacific Northwest. Ingredients like salmon, shellfish, seafood, grass-fed beef, and more exotic produce like moose, elk, caribou, along with wild mushrooms are widely used to create culinary masterpieces. The philosophy is to use the best fresh locally produced ingredients and to prepare them as simply as possible.

 *On a trip through Deception Pass with friends, we stopped at the unassuming Shrimp Shack and had the best Dungeness crab ever! Brooks, visiting from abroad and a first-time crabeater, was covered in delicious sauce by the time we left. The Shrimp Shack has been in the same family since 1973, and since then it has become renowned for serving some of the tastiest seafood dishes around.*

Facts and Statistics of the Pacific Northwest

This must be one of the regions in the United States with the most diverse climate; due to rainforests and deserts nestled between the volcanic mountain ranges. The area has several active volcanoes, most of which are in the Cascade Mountain Range. Mount Saint Helens is the most well-known, erupting on May 27, 1980, causing a 5.1-magnitude earthquake and a massive landslide. This was followed by an air blast that carried superheated ash for approximately 15 miles. The mudslides and magma flow changed this landscape forever.

A fun fact is that 60% of all apples in the United States are grown in Washington (Washington State University, 2015). Apple orchards take up around 175,000 acres of land in the state. Washington also grows a large number of pears, sweet cherries, nectarines, apricots, plums, and peaches. This makes fruit farming an important part of the state's gross domestic product (GDP).

Something else you may not know about the Pacific Northwest is that beneath the waters of Riffe Lake in Lewis County, Washington, there lie three towns. The towns of Kosmos, Nesika, and Riffe were there where it is now water. The man-made lake was built in the 1960s, and around 1,500 people lived in the towns affected. When the water level is low enough, the skeletal remains of Kosmos can still be seen.

How to Use This Book

Each of the three states, Washington, Oregon, and Idaho, in the Pacific Northwest will be covered in a separate chapter.

In every chapter, there will be "travel tips" provided that suggest travel routes, park passes, and permits, packing recommendations and ideal visiting times.

Each state, Washington, Oregon, and Idaho will be broken into **sections** with advice on how to get around, great restaurants to visit, vacation homes to rent, entertainment in the area, as well as some suggested outdoor and water recreation nearby.

For example:

- Chapter 2 - Washington State
    - Section 1 – **Northwest**
        - Restaurants, cities, vacation rentals, outdoor and water recreation, etc.
    - Section 2 – **Northeast**
        - Restaurants, cities, vacation rentals, outdoor and water recreation, etc.
    - Section 3 – **Southwest**
        - Restaurants, cities, vacation rentals, outdoor and water recreation, etc.
    - Section4 – **Southeast**
        - Restaurants, cities, vacation rentals, outdoor and water recreation, etc.

Zoom maps are also included for each of the sections in each chapter. These maps offer location references for your convenience but do not cover all suggested sites mentioned in the book. They present an easy guide for specific area planning to get you started on a fun-filled adventure-packed Pacific Northwest journey.

Please note: The Zoom maps in this book are not precisely to scale, but they provide a general idea and reference point for your ease of use in each section of the states represented.

Inside Scoop on Travel Tips for the Pacific Northwest

Pacific Northwest (PNW)
TRAVEL & IDENTIFICATION

International Travel Requirements

If you are visiting from abroad, these are the requirements:

- You will need a passport valid for six months after your travel dates.
- You will also need a visa to visit the United States issued by the Consulate or Embassy in your country.
- Another requirement may be a return ticket

If you are unsure about the rules and regulations for your country, please visit the United States Government's website (https://www.usa.gov) or contact an embassy or tourist office.

Identification Requirements

According to the Transportation Security Administration (TSA), all adult passengers flying domestically must show valid identification at the airport before they will be allowed to travel (United States Transportation Security Administration, 2019).

Acceptable identification includes:

- US passport card
- driver's license
- border crossing card
- US Department of Defense (DoD) ID
- tribal-issued photo ID
- DHS trusted traveler card
- US Merchant Mariner Credential

Pacific Northwest (PNW)
DISCOVER PASSES

Discover Passes

A Discover Pass allows vehicle access into various state parks, recreation lands and wildlife lands.

You can purchase an annual or day-use pass that offers access to more than:

- 100 state parks
- 350 recreation sites (including camping and picnic areas)
- 80 natural areas
- 30 wildlife areas

A Discover Pass is NOT required if you:

- are camping in a state park and have paid the required fee
- already have an eligible pass or permit
- only want to drive through the state recreation lands without leaving your vehicle.
- get to the recreation lands by foot, horseback, bicycle, or boat.
- visit a state park on a "free day." The free days usually fall on a holiday and details can be found at: www.discoverpass.wa.gov

The pass can be purchased online at https://www.discoverpass.wa.gov/? gclid=EAIaIQobChMI-LfOtMXI_QIVSDStBh1DVQJgEAAYASAA EgJUsvD_BwE

Chapter 2: Washington—The Evergreen State

One day, a group of tourists arrived in Seattle, eager to explore the city. As they walked around, one of them noticed a street vendor selling umbrellas. He turned to the vendor and said, "Why are you selling umbrellas on a sunny day like this?" The vendor replied with a smile, "I'm not selling umbrellas, I'm selling a souvenir from Washington State."
— Author unknown

An Overview of Washington State

Washington state is known for its stunning natural beauty, from the snow-capped peaks of the Cascade Range to the rugged coastline of the Pacific Ocean. The state also boasts lush forests, sparkling lakes, and winding rivers.

The state of Washington, named after President George Washington, shares its borders with Idaho to the east and Oregon to the south. It is divided by the majestic Cascade Mountain range. The largest population is found in the Greater Seattle region, with approximately 3.8 million people. While Seattle may have the most inhabitants, the capital city of the state is Olympia.

Of the three states in the Pacific Northwest, Washington is the smallest, with an area of around 71,400 square miles. More than half of the state is covered in trees, earning it the nickname "The Evergreen State." No wonder Washington boasts the only green flag (with a picture of George Washington). Many of the forests are planted for timber. It is no surprise that the state is a major supplier of lumber and plywood.

Mt. Rainier and Seattle, Washington

There are many reasons to visit Washington:

- Famous mountains like Mount Rainier, Mount Saint Helens, and Mount Baker, to name a few. They are magnificent whether you hike, climb, ski, or just enjoy their beauty.

- The beautiful surroundings beg to be explored and kayaking, paddleboarding, hiking, and biking are some of the activities offered in summer. Meanwhile snowboarding, skiing, and snow camping attract visitors from around the globe in winter.

- If you like the sea, this is the place to be. With more than 3,000 miles of picturesque shoreline, it is any sea lover's dream.

- One of the largest rainforests in the United States is found on the Olympic Peninsula. The Hoh Rainforest receives more than 12 feet of rain annually.

- Dunes and deserts. It may sound unbelievable, but on the other side of the Cascade Range, you will find a desert with dunes and less than 10 inches of rain annually.

- Washington offers vibrant cities like Seattle, Bellevue, Spokane, Tacoma, and even Vancouver for those travelers looking for big-city life.

- Whale watching is something not many other regions offer. In Washington, they even have an island named "Orcas Island" after the killer whales that frequent its shores.

- Fresh, healthy produce is on offer everywhere in the regions. Chefs in the area are known for cooking delicious, healthy food "from farm to table."

A fun fact is that square dancing became the state's official dance in 1979. Many people enjoy it as a fun way to exercise. Did you know that most of the apples in the United States are grown in Washington? It is home to several world-class companies, including Amazon, Microsoft, and Boeing. The Boeing factory in Everett is the largest building in the world by volume. This state has a reputation for being at the forefront of innovation in fields such as technology, aerospace, and biotechnology.

Washington is home to a diverse population, with people from all walks of life and corners of the globe. This diversity is reflected in the state's many cultural attractions. The vibrant food scene to the array of museums and galleries showcasing the work of artists from around the world is outstanding.

If you like to explore on foot, try the scenic trails near Neah Bay. There are five trails to choose from, three that run through the Makah Indian Reservation and the other two are in the Olympic National Park.

Jordan and Larisa were determined to make this hike an unforgettable adventure. They were feeling pretty confident, so they hit the trail hard! About an hour into the trek, they realized they had forgotten their trail map and compass. Undeterred, they relied on their instincts and continued to set off on their course. Things soon began to go awry and were a bit hilarious when they both slipped on a muddy patch and nearly fell. Then Larisa got chased by two squirrels who thought she was trying to steal their food. Just when they thought things could not get any crazier, they rounded a corner and came face to face with a group of hikers wearing Bigfoot costumes. So startled, they all burst out laughing and ended up taking a group photo together, making it the funniest hike of the day. It wasn't the adventure they had planned, but it was certainly one they would never forget.

"Go To" Travel Tips for Exploring Washington State

Washington
TRAVEL ROUTES

Travel & Transportation Routes in Washington

By Car
- Interstate Highways 5 and 405 connect the state from north to south.
- Interstate Highways 12, 2, 82 and 90 connect the east and west.
- Highway 101 is a major north-south highway that runs along the entire length of the West Coast of the United States.

By Train
There are many Amtrak stations in the region: https://amtrakguide.com
The three main trains are:
- Empire Builder
- Coast Starlight
- Amtrak Cascades

By Plane
There are 12 airports in Washington State that offer commercial flights. The major airport is Seattle Tacoma International.

By Bus
There are four major bus routes in the state: https://wsdot.wa.gov
- Grape Line
- Dungeness Line
- Apple Line
- Gold Line

By Ferry
This travel experience offers views of the state's rugged coastlines, waterways, and surrounding islands.

There are over ten operating routes that serve 20 terminals throughout Puget Sound, the San Juan Islands and the Olympic Peninsula.

For more information visit:
https://wsdot.wa.gov/travel/washington-state-ferries

Washington
PARK PASSES, PERMITS & BEST TIME TO VISIT

Passes & Permits

The annual <u>Northwest Forest Pass</u> allows access to the day-use of the facilities operated by the US Forest Service in Washington and Oregon.

The pass can be purchased online at https://shop.orparksforever.org/collections/park-passes/products/copy-of-annual-membership-with-northwest-forest-pass

- There are special passes and permits for hiking. Information can be found online at https://www.wta.org/go-outside/hikes.
- Washington State Parks offers discounted passes to several eligible groups: disabled veterans, people with disabilities, foster parents, and senior citizens.

Packing Suggestions

- Remember to pack an umbrella or rain jacket.
- Make sure you have comfortable shoes or hiking boots to explore hiking trails.
- You may want to pack a small backpack for a day out exploring

Best Time to Visit

<u>The best time to visit is usually between June and September</u>, when the skies are clear and the sun comes out, making it a perfect time to enjoy the outdoors.

If you enjoy skiing, snowboarding, or snowshoeing, the winter months are the perfect time to visit, from November to March.

NORTHWEST WA

NW Washington Zoom Map

Section #1 - Northwest Washington

Meet the Metro

Bellingham

Some of the best fine dining, snug cafes, and vibrant art scenes can be found in Bellingham, nestled in the scenic Bellingham Bay. This scenic city offers the following features:

- Visit the Yellow Aster Butte with views of Mount Baker and its surrounding peaks. Bellingham and the surrounding areas boast around 100,000 acres of highly fertile farmland.

- Foodies will be glad to hear that they are not left out in the cold. Seafood is featured on many menus and for the thirsty traveler, Bellingham and its surrounding area offer around 17 craft beer breweries and several wineries which use some very unique ingredients.

- Fresh air and open spaces mean adventure. Whether you want to bike, hike, run or explore the beautiful lakes via kayak, you will find something to your liking.

The San Juan Islands

The San Juan Island Archipelago has 172 small islands and over 300 miles of scenic shoreline. The three largest islands are St. Juan, Lopez, and Orcas (named after the resident pods of killer whales).

Some of the things to do on your visit:

- Several galleries and outdoor markets offer paintings, sculptures, fiber art, pottery, and jewelry for sale.

- If you love history, you can visit the Lopez Island Museum or Orcas Island Historical Museum.

- In the summer months, boating, biking, hiking, kayaking, and whale watching are available. If you like fishing, try freshwater fishing or deep-sea fishing, San Juans cater for both.

- Fresh produce is in abundance on the islands and in summertime there are regular farmers' markets where local produce can be sourced.

La Conner

The Cascade Range lies to the east and the San Juan Islands to the west, making La Conner the ideal stopover on your trip.

- While Washington winters are cold and wet, it is also the ideal time for bird watching in La Conner. Many species migrate to the area from as far away as Siberia and Alaska.

- If you visit during the first week of August with a love of cars or boats, be sure to visit the La Conner Classic Boat and Car Show. Fall has its own kind of beauty and in October it is beautiful in the Skagit Valley

Port Townsend

- The city is an art hub and a festival-goer's dream. There are all-summer-long Concerts on the Dock, the Soundcheck Music & Arts Festival, and the Port Townsend Acoustic Blues Festival.

- If you feel like having a picnic while watching the bay, head over to Chetzemoka Park. The park is close enough to both uptown and downtown Port Townsend that you can walk there. It has large gardens and a colorful rose promenade.

Seattle

As with nearly all the beautiful cities in Washington, Seattle is framed by majestic mountains known as the Cascade Range. The city itself has many outside recreational areas with pine covered mountains nearby and fresh sea air. If you're traveling with your four-legged companions, you might be interested to know that Seattle is well-known for being dog-friendly.

Seattle Wheel and Waterfront

Entrées and Edibles

Alderbrook Inn, Union

The restaurant at the Alderbrook Resort and Spa has a unique "woodland to waterfront" menu, with dishes made with ingredients from the area. Some of the dishes that caught our eye were the Alderbrook Razor Clam Chowder and the PNW Albacore Tuna. The restaurant also features an interesting beverage list with a number of hand-crafted cocktails.

The Birch Door Café, Bellingham

This quaint cafe on Meridian Street has been in the same family for three generations. It is known for its handcrafted meals and personal service. Don't walk past, knock on the Birch Door, and enjoy some good home-cooked food.

McMenamins at Elks Temple, Tacoma

The McMenamins at Elks Temple is no ordinary venue and is definitely worth a visit. The hungry can enjoy a meal at one of several restaurants, from the informal McMenamins Pub or a more upmarket restaurant, The Vault.

Nell Thorn Waterfront Bistro and Bar, La Conner

Looking for a cozy pub on the waterfront that guarantees fresh farm-to-table Northwestern cuisine? Visit Nell Thorn Bistro in La Conner. In summer, al fresco dining on the spacious deck overlooking the Swinomish Channel is not to be missed!

Pizzeria Credo, Seattle

With a five-star rating, this is your go-to for Italian food in Seattle. You can order delivery or pickup, but to have the complete experience, opt for a sit-down meal while you watch the chefs at work.

Banana Leaf Thai Bistro, Port Townsend

The restaurant is located on Washington Street, just a two-minute walk from the waterfront. The crab and shrimp wonton soup are highly recommended. For Thai food lovers with dietary restrictions, there are vegan and gluten-free dishes too.

Vacation Homes

Hillside Cabin in the Woods, Bellingham

Looking for a forest hideaway? Look no further! The 1400-square-foot cabin is built on three levels, with private rooms on each level. This self-catering home's kitchen is fully equipped to prepare delicious meals for family and friends.

Skagit Valley Farmland View Cabin, La Conner

This private log cabin in the middle of the Skagit Valley is located on a 3-acre farmland property with an 1898 Victorian farmhouse. The cabin is light and airy, with huge windows highlighting its beautiful views over the farmland.

Renovated Log Cabin, Port Townsend

The cabin sleeps four people in three well-appointed bedrooms, with sun porches for lazy afternoons and a wood stove for colder weather. The cabin is only three miles from Port Townsend.

Kangaroo House Bed and Breakfast, Orcas Island

This bed and breakfast is situated in a lodge-style home and the atmosphere is casual and known for its friendliness. Their delicious and creative breakfast, made from locally sourced ingredients, is legendary. Yes, the house is named after Josie the kangaroo, who was a resident during the 1930s, brought over from Australia by the then-owner of the house, Captain Harold (Cap) Ferris.

Kangaroo House Bed and Breakfast also offers:

- A central location in the Eastsound with easy access to restaurants, shops, and galleries
- Ensuite bathrooms in all guest rooms & an open-air hot tub in the picturesque garden
- A spacious living room with a huge stone fireplace for those cold winter evenings

Kangaroo House Bed and Breakfast, Photo by Jill McCabe

Entertainment and Tourism

Argosy Cruises, Seattle

With more than 70 years of experience in sightseeing cruises in and around Seattle, you can trust Argosy Cruises for an unforgettable experience.

- The Harbor Cruise is a one-hour excursion around Seattle; a seasoned tour guide will share facts and the history of the landmarks on the tour.
- The Locks Cruise takes 120 minutes and ventures beyond the waterfront offering a one-of-a-kind experience of going through the Hiram M. Chittenden (Ballard) Locks, also called "the boat elevator."

Seattle Center

Getting to and from the city center is easy with the many bus routes, parking spots, and the Seattle Center Monorail. The monorail travels directly between Westlake Center Mall and the Seattle Center, with departures around every 10 minutes.

- Ride the elevator to the top of the **Space Needle**. The UFO-like top floor offers glass benches leaning out over the city with the world's first (and, to date, only) revolving glass floor—not for the faint-hearted!

Space Needle, Seattle Washington

- The **Chihuly Garden and Glass** should be another stop on your visit. This long-term exhibition will delight your senses.

- **Artists at Play** is an imaginative playground created by local artists and provides free fun for all ages. There is a climbing tower, a labyrinth, and a human-powered carousel.

- For fresh produce, flowers, and unique artisan goods visit the **Pike Place Market**. It is one of the largest continuously operated public markets in the United States. It hosts hundreds of farmers, crafters, and other entrepreneurs selling their products and services.

Pikes Place Market, Seattle, Washington

i

If you ever visit Pike Place Market, you may be surprised to see "flying fish" as fish are thrown from one staff member to the next. The tradition started in the 1980s when a customer ordered a bag of clams and former owner John Yokoyama threw the bag to a colleague closer to the counter. Today visitors flock to the market to experience the spectacle. My friend Randy was one of the many visitors to the market recently. He was unaware of the tradition and accidentally stepped into a line of the fish-throwing staff. Before he could retreat, a huge Chinook was thrown his way and he spectacularly caught the specimen to everyone's delight.

- Music has been part of Seattle's culture from the start. **The Museum of Pop Culture** offers a glimpse into how music helped to shape the city.

- The young at heart should not miss a visit to the **Fremont Troll** under the Aurora Bridge. The Fremont Troll has become a Seattle celebrity. He even has his own song written about him by the Chicago band Majungas. The song is called, you guessed it, "The Fremont Troll."

- The **Seattle Art Museum** is just one block from Pike Place Market and includes exhibitions from around the world.

- The **Pacific Science Center** is located at the foot of the Space Needle. The center's vision is to ignite curiosity, and fuel a passion for discovery, experimentation, and critical thinking.

- The **Seattle Aquarium** is situated on Pier 59 and is open daily throughout the year. Some of the daily workshops include "marine animal feeding," "all about seals," and "all about our Washington waters." There is also a virtual reality swim with the whale's experience.

Krystal Acres Alpaca Farm, San Juan Islands

- This 40-acre family farm is home to 57 alpacas. The shop on the farm sells a selection of alpaca sweaters, coats, blankets, and the cutest alpaca toys.

La Conner Tulip Festival

- This town is surrounded by tulip fields, and every year, thousands of people visit the Skagit Valley for the annual tulip festival. The Tulip Frolic Parade, which is put on by the locals often has farm animals, clowns, and bands, kicking off the festival. The best time to visit is usually in April.

Seattle—Professional Sports

- Seattle Mariners Baseball
- Seattle Seahawks Football
- Kraken Hockey
- WNBA - Seattle Storm Women's Basketball
- Seattle Sounders Soccer

Other Attractions

- Chateau Ste. Michelle Winery, Woodinville
- Washington State Historical Museum, Tacoma
- Point Defiance Zoo and Aquarium, Tacoma
- Seattle Underground

Outdoor Recreation

Parks and Camping

Washington is made for adventure! The snow-capped mountains, hot springs, alpine lakes, and active volcanoes beg to be explored. The northwest region of Washington is home to three national parks, Olympic National Park, North Cascades National Park, and Mount Rainer National Park. There are numerous state parks, forests, and wilderness areas.

Deception Pass State Park

Deception Pass Park is one of the most popular parks in the region, and with good reason. The park spreads over 3,854 acres, which includes a saltwater shoreline, three lakes, and large forest areas. The park is located on two islands that are connected by Canoe Pass and Deception Pass bridges. Activities include hiking, horse trails, and water activities, including white-water kayaking. Other parks in the area worth a visit include:

- Camano Island State Park
- Birch Bay State Park
- Hope Island State Park

The Olympic National Park

The Olympic National Park is made up of nearly a million acres of wild land, such as rainforests, mountains with glaciers, and beautiful shoreline. Water is in abundance with the many rivers, lakes, and wild coastlines. Boating and fishing opportunities are very popular and continue throughout the year. There are backpacking and hiking trails all over the park, you can walk around and see a lot of nature.

Some of the most popular campgrounds include:

The **Hoh Campground** is in the Hoh Rainforest, which makes it a great place to stay. The campsite does not have RV hookups but can accommodate small RVs.

Heart O' the Hills Campground, Hurricane Ridge is nestled in the lush forests of the Olympic National Park and sits like a jewel atop the rugged peaks of Hurricane Ridge. The campsite offers breathtaking views of the surrounding mountains and valleys, with towering evergreens and babbling brooks adding to its natural charm.

Other campgrounds include:

- Sol Duc Campground
- Kalaloch Campground
- South Beach Campground
- Staircase Campground
- North Fork Campground

The North Cascades National Park

The North Cascades may be the most rugged area in the state. It is known for its majestic mountains and turquoise lakes. The scenic North Cascades Highway runs across the park and is accessible from May to November.

A great way to experience the essence of the **North Cascades National Park** is on foot. To really appreciate the majestic Cascade Range, some climbing will be involved. This area is not known as the American Alps for no reason; the towering mountains are snow capped with emerald forests on their green slopes.

Mount Baker is the highest point in the North Cascades. It has 12 glaciers and snowfields that cover 20 square miles. It can be climbed by both beginners and experts. During the winter, the area gets a lot of snow, which makes it dangerous for even the most skilled climbers to cross the crevasses.

My friend Mike, a mountaineer for many years, remembers how he climbed with a group of supposedly experienced climbers who had to turn around at the Roman Wall. This steep headwall averages around 40 degrees and is a very technical climb. So, if you plan a mountaineering trip to Mount Baker, be sure to do your homework!

The **Colonial Creek Campground** is near the shores of Diablo Lake. There are a lot of hiking trails nearby, including the famous Fourth of July Pass, which is thought to be one of the best hiking trails in the North Cascades.

Other campgrounds worth a visit include:

- Newhalem Creek Campground
- Gorge Lake Campground

- Goodell Creek Campground
- Hozomeen Campground

Treks

Some of the most beautiful hiking in the country is found in the Olympic National Park. Hiking in the mountains, near the beach, or in the forest are all options for visitors.

One of the most popular hikes is **Hurricane Ridge**, which offers fantastic views of the mountains on a clear day. Hikers can explore the winding road for 17 miles. The road ascends through dense, green forests to glacier-covered alpine peaks.
Stats: 6 miles, moderate

The **High Steel Bridge in Mason County** is a great day hike. The bridge spans a deep gorge and is the tallest railroad bridge ever built in the United States, towering 365 feet above the river. If you are not scared of heights, there are spectacular but dizzying views down into the canyon and river from the bridge.
Stats: 12-mile drive from downtown Shelton, easy

The **Staircase Rapids Loop** trail is a scenic and challenging hiking trail. The trail features steep inclines, rugged terrain, and stunning views of the surrounding wilderness. The trail offers a range of difficulty levels, from easy paths to more strenuous climbs, making it accessible for hikers of all levels.

Another hike to add to your list is the **Kendall Katwalk**, which is part of the Pacific Crest Trail. Part of the trail goes along a narrow path next to a steep rock face, which may be hard for some hikers. The trail crosses two streams, and trekking poles may be advisable. In the summer, the slopes are covered with beautiful wildflowers; you'll be able to see Lundin Peak, the Red Mountains, and Mount Rainier in the distance.

Kendall Katwalk, Snoqualmie Pass, Washington State

Stats: 14.5 miles, difficult
Rainy Lake Trail is a popular hiking trail located in the Mount Baker-Snoqualmie National Forest. The trail leads to a beautiful alpine lake nestled in the mountains. The elevation gain is about 900 feet so be ready for some uphill hiking.
Stats: 3.5 miles, moderate

One of the most scenic hikes within the park is the **Cascades Pass and Sahale Arm Trail**. This beautiful trail goes through quiet meadows on the shoulder of Sahale Mountain. The trails start at Cascade Pass, and if you visit in the summer, you will be treated to a sea of glacier lilies, while blueberries abound just before winter covers the meadows in snow.
Stats: 12 miles, easy

Other trails in the park that deserve to be mentioned are the following:

- Ladder Creek Falls trail, 1 mile, easy
- Thunder Knob trail/Diablo Lake Vista Point, 3.4 miles, moderate
- Desolation Peak Hike, 9 miles, moderate to difficult
- Skyline Divide, 7.2 miles, difficult
- Artist Ridge, 4 miles, easy
- Table Mountain, 2.4 miles, moderate
- Eldorado Peak, 8 miles, difficult
- Mount Storm King trail, 3.8 miles, difficult
- Mount Ellinor trail, 6.2 miles, moderate
- Cape Flattery trail, 1.2 miles, easy
- Grand Ridge trail and the Deer Park trail, 1.7 miles, easy

Recreation Sites

For the weary traveler, few things can be more attractive than relaxing in the waters of a hot spring. The **Sol Duc Hot Springs and Resort** in the Olympic National Forest offers three mineral hot springs and one freshwater pool. You can stay in one of the resort's rustic cabins or in one of the nearby campgrounds. The restaurant at the main lodge serves delicious meals using locally sourced ingredients; this is Northwest Cuisine at its best!

The **Snoqualmie Pass Recreation Site** offers scenic hikes in the summer, but winter sports are what the region is known for. The Summit at Snoqualmie has four base areas with unique experiences for all ability levels, making it the ideal place to hone your skills.

Fort Worden, Port Townsend offers a variety of recreational activities for visitors of all ages. One popular activity is exploring the historic fortifications and artillery batteries, providing a glimpse into the regions' military past. The beaches are perfect for swimming, sunbathing, and beach combing. The park boasts over 80 miles of hiking and biking trails.

More things to do in the region include:

- Ferry rides in the Puget Sound
- Whale watching at the San Juan Islands
- Mount Baker recreation site
- Mount Si recreation site

Water Recreation

Sailing
Pacific Northwest Sailing

Washington State's Pacific Northwest is a sailor's paradise, offering a vast array of sailing opportunities for both experienced sailors and beginners alike. One of the most popular destinations is the **San Juan Islands**, a group of over 170 islands located just off the coast of Washington State. Another great destination for sailing enthusiasts is **Puget Sound**, a deep inlet of the Pacific Ocean located in the heart of Washington. With its sheltered waters, abundant wildlife and striking scenery, Puget Sound offers some of the best sailing in the world.

For those looking for a challenge, the rugged coastline of the **Olympic Peninsula** offers exciting sailing with its open oceanwaters, rocky headland and challenging conditions.

No matter where you choose to sail in the Pacific Northwest, you'll find plenty of opportunities to explore the natural beauty of the region. From age-old forests and rocky coastlines to charming coastal towns and bustling cities, the scenery is ever changing.

There are many sailing companies that offer an inspiring adventure. A few are:

- San Juan Sailing based in Bellingham
- Milltown Sailing Association in Everett
- Seattle Sailing Club in Seattle
- Sound Experience in Port Townsend
- Northwest Sailing Adventures located in Gig Harbor
- Anacortes Yacht Charters based in Anacortes
- South Sound Sailing based in Olympia

Lakes

Diablo Lake was created when the Diablo Dam was built in the 1930s and is one of three lakes that provide electricity to nearby Seattle. The lake has a unique turquoise color, which results from suspended rock particles in the water. Activities around the lake include fishing, swimming, canoeing, and kayaking.

Lake Washington is the third deepest lake in Washington and one of the deepest lakes in the United States. You can try your hand at sailing, kayaking, stand-up paddleboarding, or even wakeboarding. The lake offers excellent fishing opportunities.

The region has many beautiful lakes. You may also want to visit:

- Crescent Lake
- Lake Cle Elum
- Lake Quinault
- Lake Sammamish

Diablo Lake, North Cascades, Washington

Waterfalls

The best time of year to visit Washington for waterfalls is in the spring, when the snow starts to thaw. Some of the most impressive waterfalls in the region can be found on the Olympic Peninsula, in Mount Rainier National Park, and in the North Bend area.

Snoqualmie Falls is breathtaking, with water plunging down cliffs that are twice as high as Niagara Falls. The falls lie within a two-acre park, and the best views of the falls are from the observation deck. The Salish Lodge is right next to the waterfalls. It has two restaurants, a gift shop, and a spa.

34

Snoqualmie Falls, Washington State

Sol Duc Falls is a picturesque waterfall that drops about 50 feet over a rocky cliff. It is surrounded by lush green forests and the area is home to a variety of wildlife. The area around the falls is crisscrossed with hiking trails offering visitors a chance to explore the Olympic National Park.

Ruby Beach, Olympic National Park, Washington State

Other waterfalls worth a visit include:

- Deschutes Waterfall
- Franklin Falls
- Granite Falls
- Whatcom Falls

Beaches

One of the most beautiful beaches in Washington must be **Ruby Beach**. The beach is well-known for its sea stacks. The beach is awash with agates, sea glass, driftwood, and seashells. The many tidepools are teeming with life, and if you are lucky, you will see starfish, spine sea urchins, anemones, and crabs.

In my opinion, one of the most relaxing things to do in the summer is to wander aimlessly on the beach. My husband, Richard, on the other hand, is one of those beachcombers looking for special finds. In the many years we have visited the Washington coastline, he has picked up numerous interesting things, from rings to watches. The strangest finds to date were dentures and bikini bottoms. I wonder how the owners coped without them.

More beaches for your list include:

- Alki Beach
- San Juan Islands
- Shi Shi Beach
- Rosario Beach
- Rialto Beach

NORTHEAST WA

NE Washington Zoom Map

Section #2 - Northeast Washington

Meet the Metro

Chelan

The city is situated in the Lake Chelan Valley. People come from all over the world to visit this city because it has a lot of outdoor activities and a thriving art scene. Outdoor activities in the summer include watersports, mountain biking, fishing, golf, and hiking. In the winter, Lake Chelan turns into a winter wonderland. Cross-country ski trails and snowshoeing in the majestic mountains give visitors a whole new experience. Whatever the season, visitors will find a range of activities.

Winthrop

You may be surprised to learn that a piece of the wild west is to be found in Winthrop, Washington. Its downtown area is designated to look like a 19-century western frontier town, complete with wooden boardwalks and hitching posts. The town is the gateway to the North Cascades National Park, home to stunning mountain scenery. Opportunities abound for biking, fishing, and horseback riding. It also has the bragging rights to one of the largest ski resorts in North America, the Methow Valley Ski Resort, offering over 120 miles of cross-country skiing trails.

Spokane

The city is the smallest ever to host the world's fair and is easily accessible. There are countless restaurants and venues in downtown Spokane, as well as a busy nightlife. Town center has buildings that are mostly charming historic structures. Visitors flock to the numerous lakes around the city to fish, boat, or swim. The region offers visitors five excellent ski resorts.

Spokane Tower, Spokane, Washington

Leavenworth

This quaint Bavarian-themed village lies in the Cascade Mountains. Front Street Park is the heartbeat of the town, bustling with shops, galleries, and restaurants. Bring the family to the Reindeer Farm, which provides tours and educational experiences. In winter, Leavenworth Ski Hill is the central location for many winter activities. Families flock to the area to ski, snowboard, and snowshoe.

Leavenworth, Washington

Wenatchee

This city is the seat of Chelan and lies in the foothills of the Cascade Range offering a plethora of activities for visitors. It is a popular destination for outdoor fanatics, with its proximity to the Cascade Mountains providing opportunities for hiking, skiing, and snowboarding. The Colombia River provides opportunities for fishing, rafting, and kayaking. Wenatchee is known as the "Apple Capital of the World" due to its abundant apple orchards and other fruit production. The area's unique climate and soil conditions produce high quality grapes that are used to make award winning wines. Visitors can enjoy the wine tasting and tours while taking in the beautiful scenery of the area.

Entrées and Edibles

Kingfisher Wine Bar, Leavenworth

It is part of the Sleeping Lady Mountain Resort and serves gourmet food in a buffet-style setting. The restaurant has its own 2-acre organic garden, and the dishes are prepared from ingredients picked freshly in the garden. During the summer, customers can eat outside on the patio and enjoy the beautiful scenery. It's best to make a reservation in advance.

Baba, Spokane

This restaurant offers comfort food with a Mediterranean flavor. Dishes like lamb shank tagine or the fig-walnut stuffed quail are examples of the delicious cuisine. The restaurant is popular with visitors, and it is advisable to book in advance.

Arrowleaf Bistro, Winthrop

This neighborhood restaurant offers great food, an extensive wine list, and friendly service. Locally grown ingredients are used to make their tasty dishes, and the menu changes often to reflect the changing seasons.

Iwa Sushi and Grill, Wenatchee

This restaurant serves fresh hibachi and Asian food that will please even the pickiest eaters. Expert chefs' hand-make fresh sushi and sashimi. Try some of the sake' beverages or enjoy a local wine with your meal.

County Line, Chelan

The restaurant offers indoor/outdoor seating. Food is made from scratch using local produce. Some of the interesting dishes include Woodin Noodle Salad or the Smoked Mac and Cheese. Bring the family, you won't leave hungry.

Vacation Homes

Romantic Riverfront Cottage, Winthrop

The knotty pine cottage is right on the Chewack River and is the perfect place for a romantic getaway in nature. Explore the nearby Pearrygin Lake State Park, the Lost River Winery, or the Confluence Gallery and Art Center.

Methow Suite Bed adruhe east slopes of the North Cascades Mountains are home to the town of Twisp and the Methow Suites. This family-friendly bed and breakfast aims to provide rest, relaxation, and rejuvenation. The rooms all have a deck and a small sitting area. The delicious Methow breakfast is served in the dining room with scenic views over the nearby mountains.

Entertainment and Tourism

Spokane Hoopfest, 3on3 Tournament

The Spokane Hoopfest is the largest 3on3 basketball tournament on earth, with nearly 6,000 teams and more than 24,000 players using 422 courts to play around 14,000 games. The event takes place annually in June and offers categories for children, teens, and adults. During the event, 45 blocks of Spokane are shut down, and 3,000 local volunteers are involved. It continues to grow exponentially and is now a highly anticipated event that attracts players and spectators from all over the world. In addition to the tournament, there are several other events, like a slam dunk contest and a free throw shooting contest. It has a tremendous effect on the community by partnering with local businesses and organizations to raise money for various charities and causes.

Grand Coulee Dam

The Grand Coulee Dam offers a variety of guided tours that provide an in-depth look at the history and operation of the dam. You can learn of the construction, the people who built it and the engineering behind it. The dam offers a nightly laser light show during the summer months. A dazzling display of lights, lasers, and music projected onto the dam's face. It is a beautiful and unique experience that's not to be missed. Don't leave without checking the visitor's center with all its exhibits, videos and displays that provide a wealth of information about the surrounding area.

Gorge Amphitheater

The Gorge Amphitheater can seat around 20,000 people and is one of America's premier outdoor concert venues. The rural town of George is situated above the Columbia River gorge, which is up to 4,000 feet deep in places and stretches for over 80 miles. There is a campground next to the Gorge for concert-goers that offers lodging.

More entertainment options in the area include:

- Washington State Apple Blossom Festival, Wenatchee
- Pigout in the Park, Spokane
- Chelan Pro-Rodeo, Chelan
- Omak Stampede, Colville Tribes
- Village of Lights Winter Carnival, Leavenworth
- Northwestern Museum of Arts and Culture, Spokane
- Lake Chelan Wine and Jazz Festival
- Colville Indian Reservation

Outdoor Recreation

State Parks and Camping

If you visit Spokane, be sure to make time for **Riverside State Park**. The park offers a huge variety of activities, including mountain biking, horseback riding, rock climbing, and many hiking trails. Bring your own horse and stay in the horse-friendly campground equipped with a riding arena and round pen. The Bowl and Pitcher is a popular place to camp in the park. It has 16 standard campsites and 13 partial hookup sites. Off-road

vehicle drivers can test their skills in the 600 acres of special terrain. Lake Spokane offers boating and angling opportunities. In winter, snowshoeing, cross-country skiing, and snowmobiling attract visitors from all around.

Pearrygin Lake State Park is situated in the Methow Valley and covers an area of over 1200 acres. The lake offers a range of recreational activities, including camping, hiking, fishing, swimming, boating and wildlife watching. The park features two campgrounds, over 11 miles of hiking trails and a 176-acre lake that is stocked with rainbow trout and kokanee salmon.

Also worth a visit:

- Lake Wenatchee State Park
- Lincoln Rock State Park
- Mount Spokane State Park
- Stehekin Valley Campground
- Bowl & Pitcher Campground

Treks

The region offers more than 1,286 miles of hiking on 25 recommended routes. Hikers have 185 easy, 920 intermediate, and 156 difficult trails to choose from (Hiking Project, 2023).

The Enchantments Traverse near Leavenworth is an extraordinary hike with a "difficult" rating. The route stretches over 19 miles and offers lovely views of nearly all the peaks in the area. It includes grueling climbs and challenging mountain passes.
Stats: 18 miles, difficult

Other hikes in the area you may consider are:

- Slate Peak Hike, 6.2 miles, difficult
- Maple Pass Loop Hike, 7.2 miles, moderate
- Blue Lake Trail, 4.5 miles, moderate
- Mount Spokane State – Summit Trail, 5.5. mile, moderate
- Kettle Crest Trail, 89 miles, difficult

North Cascade National Park

Cascade Mountains, Washington

The Cascade Loop, a 440-mile route that winds through Washington, is another experience not to be missed. There are plenty of hiking opportunities around the loop, from short scenic strolls to steep hikes and climbs. Hikers and backpackers visit the park throughout the year, but the most popular times are in the summer and spring. Some of the higher-elevation trails may have snow into July, which may limit accessibility. There are 140 designated sites that provide a low-impact camping experience to backpackers with a flat tent pad, water, and composting toilet. Hikers are not allowed to camp or sleep anywhere on the trails apart from these areas. Cross-country camping is allowed as long

as it is at least half a mile from any trail and a mile away from camping grounds.

Take a road trip along the Cascade Loop and be sure to take a byway for a memorable experience. Three byways in the loop are:

- **Stevens Pass Greenway**, stretching from Monroe in Snohomish County to Peshastin in Chelan Country.
- **North Cascades Byway**, from Twisp in the Methow Valley to Sedro-Woolley in the Skagit Valley.
- **Whidbey Scenic Isle Way** spans the length of the island providing access to beaches, trails, and charming towns. (Located in the northwest section of Washington)

There are plenty of water sports, from boating (bring your own or rent one) to fishing, swimming, and paddle boarding. If you are planning to fish in one of the rivers or lakes, be sure to purchase your fishing license in advance. The more adventurous visitors can get their adrenaline pumping while rafting down one of the rivers in the area with a professional river guide.

If you love watching the stars, you will want to book a space at the Coyote Estates Campsite. The site is on top of a mountain plateau and offers a flawless view of the stars and the Milky Way. Remember to bring your telescope or camera with a good lens along!

Depending on the season, you can expect to see a variety of wildlife.

Big Horn Sheep, Cascade Mountains, Washington

Species often seen include:

- black bears
- bighorn sheep
- mountain goats

Lake Chelan, Washington

Water Recreation

Lakes

Lake Chelan, this beautiful region offers more than 300 days of sunshine, a crystal-clear lake, vineyards, mountains, and charming villages. In the summer, the lake teems with activity, while in the winter it has a different magic when the landscape transforms into a snowy wonderland. Fall is spectacular as the vineyards change color, while spring brings sunshine and meadows of wildflowers. Whatever the time of year, you will not be disappointed when you visit!

Other lakes in the area include:

- Lake Wenatchee
- Banks Lake
- Sullivan Lake
- Franklin Roosevelt Lake

Waterfalls

There are very few things that can match a waterfall's breathtaking splendor. You have to go far to beat the beauty of **Spokane Falls**. Located in Riverfront Park, the falls is a series of cascading waterfalls and channels which help direct the Spokane River flow and create a scenic background for visitors. The falls are at their

prettiest in spring when snow from the mountains feeds the streams and rivers. Viewing spots are easily accessible due to the number of bridges and walkways that offer spectacular water displays.

Spokane Falls at Riverfront Park, Spokane, Washington

Other falls in the area include:

- Dry Falls Waterfall
- Rainbow Falls
- Bridal Veil Falls
- Crown Point Falls

Rivers

The **Wenatchee River** has its origins at Lake Wenatchee before it flows to the city of Leavenworth. The many fruit orchards and vineyards are dependent on the flow of the river. Human activity also centers around the river and the activities it provides; swimming, fishing, rafting, and kayaking are popular during the summer months.

The **Spokane River**, a tributary of the **Columbia River**, begins at Lake Coeur d'Alene in Idaho and merges with the Columbia River at Lake Roosevelt. The mighty Columbia River cuts through the Cascade Mountains to form the border between Washington and Oregon. The gorge formed by the river eroding away the mountains is as deep as 4,000 feet in places, and it is reckoned as one of the six natural wonders of Washington

Columbia River, Washington

SOUTHWEST WA

SW Washington Zoom Map

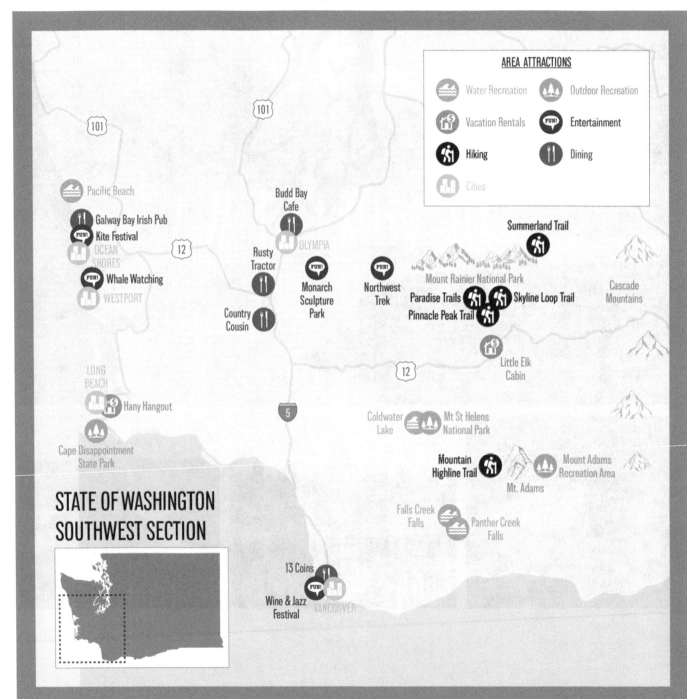

AREA ATTRACTIONS

Water Recreation
Outdoor Recreation
Vacation Rentals
Entertainment
Hiking
Dining
Cities

Pacific Beach
Galway Bay Irish Pub
Kite Festival
OCEAN SHORES
Whale Watching
WESTPORT

Budd Bay Cafe
OLYMPIA
Rusty Tractor
Monarch Sculpture Park
Country Cousin

Northwest Trek

Summerland Trail
Mount Rainier National Park
Paradise Trails
Skyline Loop Trail
Pinnacle Peak Trail
Cascade Mountains

Little Elk Cabin

LONG BEACH
Hany Hangout
Cape Disappointment State Park

Coldwater Lake
Mt St Helens National Park

Mountain Highline Trail
Mount Adams Recreation Area
Mt. Adams

Falls Creek Falls
Panther Creek Falls

13 Coins
Wine & Jazz Festival
VANCOUVER

STATE OF WASHINGTON SOUTHWEST SECTION

Section #3 - Southwest Washington

Meet the Metro

Ocean Shores

This beach town is situated in Grays Harbor County. Sandy beaches, excellent restaurants, and freshwater canals for boating — even more fun, visit the Ocean Shores Kite Store. The store sells kites, windsocks, and yard spinners.

Apart from the beach, there are many things to do. Gallop across the sandy beaches on a trusty steed or rent a moped and explore the neighboring countryside. Play mini-golf, laser tag, or one of the many arcade games available for family fun.

Long Beach

Long Beach is the starting point for the Long Beach Peninsula, which is the longest stretch of beach on the west coast with 28 miles of clean sand. This area is known for having a lot of sea life, the largest salmon run in the world, and many kinds of fish, such as halibut, cod, sardines, tuna, and anchovies. The waters also teem with razor clams and oysters.

Westport

This family-friendly town is one of the best-kept secrets in the Northwest. Sandy beaches, excellent seafood, and a museum dedicated to mermaids. If you like fishing, why not enter the annual Westport Charter Boat Association Derby? This locally sponsored event takes place throughout the season and draws fishermen from all over the world who compete to catch the largest chinook (king) salmon. There are daily and weekly prizes, everyone stands the chance of winning something.

Seagull attack, Washington Beaches, Photo by Romy Hoffman

If you thought that only seasoned fishermen win prizes, you would be wrong! One of Mick's favorite stories is about the day he and his fiancée chartered a boat in Westport. They had never fished before but were very excited to catch their own supper. The third time Mick threw out his line, he got a bite and struggled to get the huge salmon aboard. To everyone's surprise, Mick had made the catch of the day! Their prize money covered their stay for the weekend, and they have been back many times. I must add that the fish gets bigger every time Mick tells the story!

47

Vancouver

This lively city with a small-town feel is on the banks of the Columbia River. It has beautiful nature parks with views of the mountains, an exciting downtown with tasty restaurants, a lively art scene, and miles of bike trails. Vancouver's historic waterfront offers luxury hotels, trendy shops, and unique eateries.

Olympia

Olympia, apart from being the official capital, Olympia is known for being a cultural hub and a popular stopover for visitors on their way to the ocean. Olympia has many stunning parks, interesting museums, galleries, and an inviting waterfront.

Entrées and Edibles

Galway Bay Irish Pub, Ocean Shores

This loved pub is a cozy spot that serves up some delicious Irish-inspired cuisine. One of the standout dishes is Shepherd's Pie. Don't forget to try their smooth selection of Irish beers and whiskeys to complete the experience.

13 Coins Restaurant, Vancouver

This restaurant offers 24-hour service and a classic ambiance that inspires a strong sense of satisfaction. Some standout options are the Crab Cakes, and the 13 Coins Burger, a customer favorite! You will find something delicious on the menu at this classic American restaurant.

Budd Bay Café, Olympia

Budd Bay is known for its commitment to serving fresh, sustainable seafood and locally sourced ingredients. The menu features a variety of seafood dishes, meat, and vegetarian options. The restaurant derives its name from Budd Bay in Olympia, the same location where it's situated. This little tidbit adds a special touch of local charm to the dining experience.

Country Cousin Restaurant, Centralia

This family-owned restaurant offers a wide range of comfort foods, like pot roasts and a variety of fried dishes. The restaurant also offers a diversely filled country store.

The Rusty Tractor Family Restaurant, Elma

An absolute favorite with visitors to Greys Harbor for its delicious food and friendly service. Try the Rusty Tractor Special, one of the famous breakfast options. On the dinner menu, the Admiral's Platter is a top favorite. For those with a sweet tooth, the Apple Doodle, a homemade apple cobbler with a cookie topping, should be on the list.

Vacation Homes

Little Elk Cabin, Packwood

If you are planning a ski outing to Mount Rainier and the White Pass Ski Area, this freshly remodeled cabin is the ideal place to stay. The cabin boasts a hot tub for relaxing and is pet-friendly, so you can take your furry friend along on hikes in the nearby forests.

Hany Hangout, Long Beach

The large vacation home sleeps eight people in three spacious bedrooms. It is centrally located within walking distance of the beach, restaurants, and shops. The house is fully equipped and even has two adult bicycles for guests to use in the garage.

Entertainment and Tourism

Vancouver Wine and Jazz Festival

Festivals are all the rage during the summer months, and visitors have quite a wide variety of choices. One of the festivals that should be at the top of your list is the Wine and Jazz Festival in Vancouver. At the festival, there are many commercial booths, hundreds of wines, and a lot of local restaurants. There are also artists like Grace Kelly, Kenny Loggins, and Los Lobos to name just a few that have graced the stage of this world-class event.

Kite Festival, Ocean Shores

The seaside town of Ocean Shores bursts into color as the Kite Festival gets underway the first full weekend of June. During the festival, there are kite-making classes for the children and mass kite-flying events.

A few years ago, we visited Ocean Shores over the weekend with family, and my niece begged for a red "dazzling diamond" kite. Soon after we arrived, she discovered the kite store. Her mom gave in on day two, and Rachael spent the rest of the weekend at the beach. Just before we had to depart, she insisted on one last visit to the beach and was so desperate to make this last chance count that she did not hold on tightly enough. You guessed it, the precious kite flew free. We all expected tears, but instead, she was so excited to see how high her kite could fly, and we all stood watching and waving until it disappeared into the blue cloudless sky.

Northwest Trek Adventures, Tacoma

Meet the animals of the Northwest up close at this unique wildlife park. Explore the park on foot by following the animal walking path. You will get up close to bears, foxes, several species of wild cats, and wetland inhabitants like otters, beavers, and badgers. The park boasts of 435-acres to discover herds of elk, caribou, deer, and bison. Remember to buy your artisan souvenir at the gift shop!

Whale Watching, Westport

Every year, approximately 23,000 whales migrate through this area, and many people consider it a bucket-list experience. Westport is one of the most popular places to go whale watching, and many charter boats offer trips every spring. Apart from the majestic gray whales, visitors can expect to also see humpback whales and harbor porpoise that also frequent the waters.

More things to do in the Southwest include:

- The Peninsula Arts Center, Long Beach
- Cranberry Festival, Grayland
- Monarch Sculpture Park, Tenino
- Tokeland Wood and Art Festival
- Vancouver Waterfront
- Fort Vancouver National Historic Site
- End of the World Rod Run, Long Beach
- Longmire Museum, Mount Rainier

Outdoor Recreation

State Parks and Camping

Around 50 miles north of Portland, you will find **Mount St. Helens**, one of several volcanic mountains in the region but the only one to have erupted in recent history. On May 18, 1980, a 5.1-magnitude earthquake caused the mountain to erupt with a huge avalanche of debris. The area is known as Mount St. Helens National Volcanic Monument and is divided into three visiting areas, each with trails, viewpoints, and camping grounds.

The Pacific Ocean and the Columbia River meet at **Cape Disappointment State Park**. Steep cliffs dotted with lighthouses are not all this park offers. There are also mature forests, freshwater lakes, and saltwater marshes. The area is known as a fishing destination, with salmon, crab, and clams in abundance.

Other parks to visit include:

- Millersylvania State Park
- Paradise Point State Park
- Battleground State Park
- Mowich Lake Campground
- Cougar Rock Group Campground
- Sunrise Campground
- White River Campground
- Big Creek Campground

Treks

Mount Rainier National Park

The park is broken up into five sections, each with its own entrance to the park.

These regions are:

- **Paradise**, which is on the southern side of the mountain and is known for its stunning nature and gorgeous wildflowers. If your time in the park is limited, we recommend spending it in this region.

- **Longmire** is home to the park's historic district in the southwestern portion. The area is known for its dense forests, and log cabins.

- **Carbon River/Mowich Lake** has some of the best hiking and camping in the park, but beware the access road, which requires skillful driving.

- **Ohanapecosh** region in the southeast corner of the park has some of the best ancient woodlands. If you feel like escaping the summer crowds, head this way!

- **Sunrise** and is a very popular region in the northeastern part, mostly due to the stunning views of Mount Rainier.

The park is dotted with picnic spots, some close to thundering waterfalls. The more adventurous will find plenty of rock climbing and mountaineering opportunities in the park. During the snowy winter months, snowshoeing trails attract enthusiasts.

Summerland Hike in Mount Rainier National Park offers scenic meadows and beautiful waterfalls at the base of Mount Rainier, which stands 14,411 feet tall. The hike takes between three and five hours, and the Summerland Camp offers the ideal lunch spot on the way. For a harder hike, keep going up to the Panhandle Gap, where you can see beautiful views of the amphitheaters and the tall Mount Rainier.
Stats: 8.4 miles, moderately difficult

Another trail in Mount Rainier National Park is the **Wonderland Trail**, which travels 93 miles around Mount Rainier. Hikers are required to have an overnight permit before starting out. Hikers are allowed a maximum of 14 days to complete the 93 miles. The trek is strenuous and has lots of ups and downs, and your skill and fitness level will determine the distance between campsites.
Stats: 93 miles, difficult

Mount Rainier, Washington

Mount Adams Recreation Area

Mount Adams recreation area spans over 21,000 acres and has nine named mountains, the most prominent being Mount Adams. Some of the best hikes in the area include the **Little Mount Adams** and **Bird Creek Meadows** trails, as well as the **Mountain Highline Circuit**, which connects the three existing trails. A four-mile section called "The Gap" must be crossed by hikers. This section requires a lot of mountaineering skills and is not for casual hikers.
Stats: 9.4 miles, moderately difficult

Other hikes in the area worth mentioning include:

- Skyline Loop, 5.5 miles, moderate to strenuous
- Naches Peak Loop, 3.5 miles, moderate
- Pinnacle Peak, 3.5 miles, moderate
- Glacier Basin, 3.6 miles, moderate
- Myrtle Falls Trail, 0.88 miles, easy

Photo by Romy Hoffman

Water Recreation

Wind Surfing

The **Columbia River Gorge** is a popular place for windsurfing. Its consistently strong winds make it one of the best places in the world for windsurfing. The narrow canyon that runs through the Cascade Mountains, creating a natural wind tunnel that funnels the wind from the coast through the gorge. The prevailing airstream in the gorge is from the west, and it can be quite strong ranging from 15 to 35 knots on average. There are several launch sites along the Columbia River, including Hood River, Stevenson, and The Wall.

Other locations popular in Washington for wind surfing include:

- Westport Jetty in Westport and Lake Wenatchee in central Washington
- Jetty Island located in Everett, northwest part of Washington
- Lake Washington in Seattle, northwest part of Washington

Lakes

A very popular picnic and boating site is found at **Coldwater Lake**. It was formed when Mount Helens erupted as a volcano in 1980.

Other lakes in the area that should be on your list are:

- Alder Lake
- Vancouver Lake
- Silver Lake
- Lake Sacajawea
- Yale Lake
- Mineral Lake

Waterfalls

Falls Creek Falls is a 335-foot-tall waterfall that drops in multiple tiers. On the upper tier is a powerful 200-foot drop cascading over a rocky cliff face. On the lower tier is a gentler 35-foot drop that spills into a serene pool below.

Panther Creek Falls is accessible via a short easy hike through the forest. The path has a series of wooden steps and footbridges to help hikers navigate. The falls consist of a 50-foot drop flowing down a rocky cliff face into a tranquil pool below. The waterfall is surrounded by lush forest and ferns making a picturesque site. The pool below is a favored swimming spot during warmer months.

Other waterfalls in the area that should be on your list are:

- Lower Lewis River Falls
- Spirit Falls
- Curly Creek Falls
- Dougan Falls

Beaches

The **Long Beach Peninsula** is a 28-mile stretch of sandy beaches. The beaches are uncrowded, and the Long Beach Boardwalk stretches for half a mile from the city with striking views of the ocean. The peninsula is also home to no fewer than six state parks, of which one is a treasure yet undiscovered by the crowds.

Seabrook is one of the newer beach developments and offers miles of coastline for beachcombing and tide pooling. During low tide guests can discover sea anemones, starfish, crabs, and other marine life. It is a great location for biking on the many trails and bike friendly roads.

Other beaches in the area you may want to include in your visit are:

- Ocean Shores
- Pacific Beach
- Ocean Park Beach
- Westport Beach

Washington Beaches, Photo by Romy Hoffman

SOUTHEAST WA

SE Washington Zoom Map

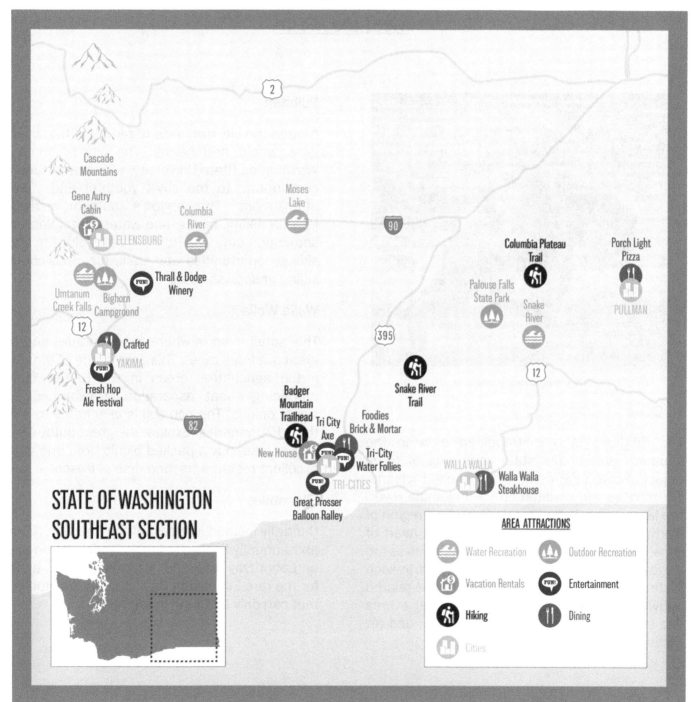

Cascade Mountains

Gene Autry Cabin

ELLENSBURG

Columbia River

Moses Lake

90

Thrall & Dodge Winery

Umtanum Creek Falls

Bighorn Campground

12

Crafted

YAKIMA

Fresh Hop Ale Festival

82

Columbia Plateau Trail

Palouse Falls State Park

Snake River

395

12

Snake River Trail

Porch Light Pizza

PULLMAN

Badger Mountain Trailhead

Tri City Axe

Foodies Brick & Mortar

New House

Tri-City Water Follies

WALLA WALLA

Walla Walla Steakhouse

TRI-CITIES

Great Prosser Balloon Ralley

STATE OF WASHINGTON SOUTHEAST SECTION

AREA ATTRACTIONS

Water Recreation

Outdoor Recreation

Vacation Rentals

Entertainment

Hiking

Dining

Cities

Section #4 - Southeast Washington

Meet the Metro

Ellensburg Rodeo, Washington

Tri Cities

The Tri-Cities is a metropolitan area in the southern part of the state consisting of three adjacent cities: Kennewick, Pasco, and Richland. These cities are situated on the Columbia River, the largest river in the Pacific Northwest region of North America. The Tri-Cities are in the heart of wine country with more than 200 wineries in the surrounding area. Visitors can take part in wine tastings, vineyard tours and other wine-related activities. Richland offers many cultural events like symphonies, ballets, medieval fairs, and art festivals.

Pullman

Around the city are miles of farmland that mostly grow wheat and beans. The city is home to Washington State University, with many students contributing to the city's youthful and vibrant atmosphere. The region's outdoor activities include hiking, biking, and watersports. Winter is snow sport time with Pullman being close to many skiing opportunities and trails for cross-country skiing or snowshoeing.

Walla Walla

This small town is where wine, culture, and the great outdoors meet. This area is one of the most fertile agricultural areas in the United States producing wheat, asparagus, strawberries, and sweet onions. The rich soil is also home to more than 120 wineries. Explore the great outdoors on foot or bike, buy a packed picnic from one of the excellent restaurants, and dine al fresco.

Ellensburg

Centrally located just east of the Cascade Range, and annually hosts the largest rodeo in the state on Labor Day weekend. The town is also known for the rare Ellensburg Blue, a beautiful blue gem that can only be found in the region.

Washington Vineyards

Yakima

This town is in the wine country and is known as the place where Washington's wine industry began. Explore the 17,000-acre vineyards and enjoy exceptional wine tasting with renowned winemakers. The fertile soil is home to more than 3,000 farms producing a huge variety of produce. There are plenty of outdoor activities to enjoy.

Entrées and Edibles

Drumheller's Food and Drink, Tri-Cities

This elegant restaurant is in the Lodge at Columbia Point and is frequented by both locals and tourists. The menu is seasonal and dependent on locally sourced ingredients.

Foodies Brick and Mortar, Tri-Cities

A family-owned restaurant that prides itself on providing the best food and an inviting atmosphere. The restaurant is also renowned for its delicious cakes and desserts. Sit down or take out—the choice is yours!

PorchLight Pizza, Pullman

Hand-crafted, fast-fired pizza for sit-down or takeout. The restaurant is known for its unique pizza options. Patrons can also choose to build their own pizza by combining the unique ingredients.

Walla Walla Steak Company

This is a steakhouse with a difference and offers award-winning food in the historic train depot in downtown Walla Walla. The restaurant has many events taking place throughout the year. On the menu, you can find local favorites like Dungeness crab and signature steaks that can be cooked to your liking.

Crafted, Yakima

This restaurant offers simple, seasonal, and delicious farm-to-table dishes. On the menu, there are several items that can be ordered individually or as part of a multi-course meal for the whole table. Dishes that catch the eye include wood-fired salmon served with a garlic-chive aioli.

Vacation Homes

Gene Autry Cabin, Thorp (Ellensburg)

The cabin is on a 20-acre ranch where horses and pets are welcome. The cabin comfortably fits a family of four, and horses and dogs are welcome to use the barn space provided to guests.

New house! A hot tub and a firepit await you (Kennewick)

The brand-new modern house offers a cozy living room with a fireplace. The outdoor space offers a hot tub on the patio and a firepit in the manicured garden. It's in the middle of everything, and close to great restaurants, shops, and the Southridge Sports Complex.

Entertainment and Tourism

Great Prosser Balloon Rally, Prosser

Prosser is a charming little town on the banks of the Yakima River. Hot air balloons have taken to the sky annually in September since 1991. Balloon pilots from all over the Northwestern United States converge to fly their balloons in the rally. The Night Glow Show kicks off the rally, where visitors can not only meet the pilots but also buy balloon memorabilia while being entertained by local musicians.

We were fortunate enough to be invited by one of the pilots to join him on a hot air balloon trip. It was one of the most enjoyable experiences we have ever had. It took our breath away (literally from anticipation) as we slowly ascended into the sky.

Our excitement continued as we glided above the green vineyards and orchards below, following the Yakima River as it wound through the valley. We caught glimpses of wildlife, deer and some birds that call the valley home. In the distance we saw the Cascade Mountains, creating a stunning background for our balloon ride. The feeling of gently riding the breeze and the beautiful landscape below is something we will always treasure.

Thrall and Dodge Winery, Ellensburg

Hot Air Balloons, Prosser, Washington

This winery is the oldest farm winery in the Kittitas Valley. This farm is known as the "fruit bowl" of the valley, orchards and vineyards abound. The winery has scenic views of the Stuart Mountain range, which can be enjoyed while tasting wine during the summer months.

Tri-Cities Water Follies

The Water Follies, the biggest weekend festival in the area, is fun for people who like speed and water. Hydroplanes reading up to 220 miles per hours compete against each other in different classes. Every year, the festival draws crowds of up to 50,000 people. If you are in the vicinity at the end of July, don't miss out on this unique experience!

A hydroplane pilot, Greg, shared a funny story with us about a friend with a very inflated view of himself named Ethan. He had expressed a desire to ride with Greg in a hydroplane and "just had to experience the speed." Greg hesitantly agreed to have him as a passenger in one of the warm-up heats. Ethan arrived in the morning full of bluster, telling everyone within hearing distance that he drives a sports car and is used to speeds much faster than what you can do on water. By the time Greg and Ethan had climbed into the hydroplane, Greg, tired of hearing about Ethan's fast cars and great driving experiences suddenly pulled away, causing Ethan to lose his balance and land like a sack of potatoes in his seat. They were surrounded by other pilots and the mishap did not go unnoticed. Laughter and shouting comments about water speed being different from land speed were galore. Ethan was very quiet during the rest of the heat. Maybe he will think twice before praising his own tail in the future.

Fresh Hop Ale Festival, Yakima

It was named one of the top ten beer festivals in the country, with over 70 breweries, wineries, and cideries participating. The Yakima Valley contributes nearly two-thirds of the hops produced in the United States. The festival also offers live music, many food vendors, and loads of entertainment.

More entertainment options include:

- Fresh Bite at Johnson Orchards, Yakima
- Elson S. Floyd Cultural Center, Pullman
- The Reach Museum, Tri-Cities
- Yakima Indian Reservation
- Inside Out Community Project, Yakima

Outdoor Recreation

State Parks and Camping

Big Horn Campground is located in the heart of the Kittitas Valley, near the Yakima River, offering a variety of recreational activities, including fishing for trout, bass, and salmon, hiking, and birdwatching. The area surrounding is home to a variety of bird species, including hawks, eagles, and ospreys in their natural habitat. The campground features over 100 campsites, including both tent and RV sites, as well as several cabins.

Palouse Falls State Park provides visitors with a front-row seat to Palouse Falls, which plunges 200 feet into a rock bowl. The park offers three views of the falls. The lower viewpoint is reached by a set of steps leading directly off the parking lot, while the other viewpoints are reached via paved or gravel pathways. Visitors should take note that there is no phone service in the park, but staff is on hand in case of emergencies. Day visitors can use a picnic shelter, open-air barbecues, 15 picnic tables, and 2 acres of open space for picnicking.

Bear Lake Campground is located in the Okanogan-Wenatchee National Forest, near the town of Naches. It is a popular destination for camping, hiking, fishing, and wildlife viewing. The area is home to a variety of wildlife, including black bears, deer, and elk. The campsites are near the lake and offer beautiful views of the nearby mountains.

As the sun began to set on the horizon, Tim and Hayley set up their tents near tranquil Bear Lake. They had noticed signs of bear activity in the area and were a bit nervous but thrilled at the prospect of encountering one of these magnificent creatures. As they sat round the campfire, enjoying the warm glow of the flames, they heard a rustling in the bushes nearby. Suddenly, a black bear emerged from the shadows, its nose twitching as it sniffed the air. The two froze, watching in awe as the bear ambled towards them before pausing to scratch its back against a nearby tree. After a few moments, the bear lost interest and disappeared back into the forest. The two let out a collective sigh of relief, exhilarated by the close encounter with one of nature's most impressive predators.

Other parks that you may want to visit include:

- Potholes State Park
- Lewis and Clark State Park
- Steptoe Battlefield State Park
- Elk Ridge Campground near Yakima

Treks

Lower Snake River Trail is a multi-use trail that follows the Snake River. The trail is relatively flat and an easy walk. Some sections of the trail are rocky and exposed, while others are shaded by trees following the river's edge. A very scenic and rewarding hike suitable for all ranges of hikers.
Stats: 14 miles, easy

Columbia Plateau Trail runs through the heart of southeast Washington. The trail offers a variety of hiking and biking options from short day hikes to multi-day backpacking trips.
Stats: 130 miles, easy

Other hikes that you may want to visit include:

- Kamiak Butte, 3.5 miles, moderate
- Badger Mountain Trail, 4.4 miles, moderate
- Walla Walla River Trail, 2.2 miles, easy
- Lewis and Clark Trail, 5 miles, moderate
- Palouse Falls Trail, 1 mile, easy
- Snake River Trail, 2.3 miles, easy to moderate
- Steptoe Butte State Park – Summit Trail, 1.5 miles, easy

Recreation Sites

Outdoor and water enthusiasts in the region have a long list of possibilities. The **Yakima River** is counted among the best places for fly fishing in the state. While chinook salmon is the largest fish in the river, brown, rainbow, and cutthroat trout also grow to great size. During the fall and winter months, when the river flows more slowly, fishing on foot becomes easier with deeper runs along with more accessible pools.

Tri-Cities Axe is an indoor axe-throwing facility located in Kennewick. Individuals and groups can choose from a range of axe-throwing experiences. All the equipment including the axes, safety gear and target boards are provided. The facility also offers different game formats such as standard bullseye targets, trick shot challenges and team competitions. Give it a try as something new and adventurous.

Ice Harbor Lock and Dam are located on the Snake River near Pasco. This site offers opportunities for boating, fishing, and picnicking. There is also a visitor center for education on the building of the dam and its operation.

Located near Benton City is **Rattlesnake Slope Wildlife Area** that offers wildlife viewing and birdwatching. There are several trails that wind through the area and guests might spot some deer, coyotes, and a variety of bird species. The area is known for its rattlesnake population, so visitors are advised to watch their steps while exploring.

Other recreational activities in the area include:

- River and Lake fishing in the Columbia River, Snake River, and Potholes Reservoir
- Cliff jumping near Snake River, the Blue Mountains, or Palouse Falls State Park
- Zintel Canyon Greenway Park
- Fort Walla Walla Park

Water Recreation

Lakes

Moses Lake offers a water trail offering different experiences. The trail is designed for small, non-motorized boats like rowboats, sailboats, canoes, and kayaks to explore the waterways with unique parks along the shoreline.

Other lakes in the region include:

- Sprague Lake near Spokane
- Bonny Lake
- Bennington Lake

Waterfalls

The most well-known waterfall in the region is the majestic **Palouse Falls**, thundering 200 feet into a granite rock bowl. The falls can be seen from three viewing decks; the lower deck is only a 0.1-mile walk down a path with some steps, while the other two decks require more of a hike.

Palouse Falls, Washington

Another waterfall worth visiting is **Umtanum Creek Falls**, which is relatively easy to access. It is a spectacular waterfall that plunges approximately 50 feet from the top of a basalt cliff into a picturesque pool below. The falls is a short hike making it a great option for hikers of all skill levels.

Silver Falls is a stunning waterfall that drops approximately 40 feet in a series of cascades over moss-covered rocks. The falls are easily accessible via a short trail from the Ohanapecosh Campground. They are enclosed by a lush, forested area, surrounded by tall trees and ferns. Visitors to the falls enjoy hiking trails, picnic areas and impressive views of the surrounding landscape.

Other waterfalls in the area include:

- Tucannon Falls
- White Salmon Falls
- Mill Creek Falls
- Snake River Falls

Rivers

The three main rivers in the region are the Columbia, the Yakima, and the Palouse River. These rivers have significant cultural, economic, and ecological importance to the local communities. The **Palouse River** is a popular spot for fishing and recreation, while the **Yakima River** is an important source of irrigation for agriculture. The **Columbia River** is a major transportation artery for goods and services which supports a variety of fish and wildlife. All three rivers are part of the larger Columbia River watershed, which encompasses over 260,000 square miles and extends into seven US states along with one Canadian province. The watershed is home to over 14 million people. All of these rivers offer parks, campgrounds, and water recreation.

Other rivers in the area include:

- Snake River
- Walla Walla River
- Touchet River

Mid-Book Review Page

Travel is the passport to expand your horizons ignite your soul and create
memories that last a lifetime."
-Rick Steves

Within the pages of this book, you have already discovered the allure of the Pacific Northwest – a land that beckons you with its unique wonders, breathtaking beauty, a way to appreciate life, and find solace in our surroundings.

And now I invite you to share your own journey through the pages of the Pacific Northwest Travel Guide & Stories.

By offering your review, you have the opportunity to improve the lives of others by sharing the benefits of travel and the joy of creating memories with loved ones.

Simply convey to others what they can expect within the pages of this travel adventure book – a passport to discovering hidden gems, uncovering local secrets, and immersing oneself in the splendor of the Pacific Northwest. Your effort in sharing this resource will encourage travelers to share in the appreciation of nature, exploration, and family.

Offer a review by scanning the QR code or go to: bit.ly/43ypGb3

Thank you for your valuable review and now let's get back to our exciting adventures in exploring the Pacific Northwest.

May your own adventures continue to inspire and uplift.

Chapter 3: Oregon—The Beaver State

Oregon is one of the most beautiful states in the country. From its stunning coastline to its majestic mountains, it's a place that never fails to take your breath away.

-John Kitzhaber

An Overview of Oregon

Mount Hood and Portland, Oregon

Oregon takes first place as the largest state in the Pacific Northwest, with an approximate area of 98,380 square miles. This makes it the ninth-largest state in the United States. Beavers were abundant in the region, hence the nickname "The Beaver State" for Oregon.

Oregon has eight major regions, from the Oregon Coast to the Blue Mountains, each with its own unique culture, landscape, and even cuisine— eight reasons to visit! The state offers majestic mountains, wild coastlines, and parched deserts. Mount Hood is the highest peak in the state, towering 11,249 feet above the landscape. Outdoor adventures are easy to come by in this beautiful state, whether hiking, mountaineering, or biking. Mount Bachelor boasts the largest ski resort in the state, while Mount Hood offers some of the best snow sports in the state.

The state has many breathtaking parks, from Ecola State Park on the coast to Crater Lake's alpine blue water or the Columbia Gorge's wild beauty. The Oregon coast offers whale watching, while varying species of mammals call the state's mountains, prairies, and forests home. More than 500 types of birds pass through the state during spring and fall, making the region a premium bird-watching destination.

Fun facts about the state:

- Did you know that Oregon has no sales tax? Everything is on sale all the time!

- The largest number of wintering bald eagles are found in the Klamath Basin National Wildlife Refuge complex.

- There are more than 7,502 vineyards and wineries in Oregon.

- The state has the only scenic bikeway program in the nation with 17 bikeways across the state.

- You may not pump your own gas; letting an attendant pump your gas is compulsory.

- The world's smallest park is in Portland, Oregon and named Mill Ends Park. It is circular with a diameter of just two feet and is home to a single tree and some flowers. It has been named the "smallest park in the world" by the Guinness Book of World Record.
(https:// www.oregonencyclyopedia.org)

Mill Ends Park, Portland, Oregon

When Red and Boone took their mom along on an Oregon road trip it led to many moments of sheer embarrassment. Mom was not used to waiting for an attendant to pump gas for the car and they had to constantly remind her to stay seated. On more than one occasion, the silver-haired lady would jump out of the car ready to do the honor of pumping the gas for them. She also kept forgetting that there was no sales tax in Oregon. They had to hear many times about the 'bargains' she bought as the shop 'forgot' to add tax. At the time, Boone and Red did not find it funny, but now, years later, they tell the story with such gusto that you cannot help but to picture their mom insisting on pumping gas and finding bargains galore!

65

Savvy travel tips for exploring the state of Oregon

Oregon
TRAVEL ROUTES, PASSES & PERMITS

Travel & Transportation Routes in Oregon

 ### By Car
- Interstate Highways 5 connects the state from north to south.
- Interstate Highways 84 and 20 connect the east and west.

 ### By Plane
- There are five airports in Oregon that offer commercial and chartered flights.
- The most visited are Portland International Airport and Rogue Valley International-Medford Airport.

 ### By Train
There are two main railroad services in Oregon: www.amtrak.com
- Coast Starlight
- Amtrak Cascades

 ### By Bus
- The Amtrak Thruway Buses make traveling in the state a pleasure, reaching every corner of the region with regular trips daily.

Passes & Permits

- The annual Northwest Forest Pass allows day-use in Washington and Oregon.
  The pass can be purchased online at https://shop.orparksforever.org

- Permits for state park can be purchased online from https://oregonstateparks.org

Oregon
WHAT TO PACK &
BEST TIME TO VISIT

Packing Suggestions

Here are some specific items to consider packing:

- Waterproof jacket or raincoat
- Warm sweater or fleece
- Comfortable walking shoes or hiking boots
- Sunscreen and sunglasses
- Water bottle
- Hat or cap
- Swimsuit (if visiting in the summer)
- Camera or phone with camera capabilities
- Layered clothing options for different temperatures and activities
- Depending on your planned activities, you may also want to consider packing camping gear, a bike, or other outdoor equipment.

Best Time to Visit

The best time to visit will depend on what kind of experience you want.

- If you dream about snow sports, such as skiing or snowboarding, then the winter months (December to February) are the best time to visit.
- If you want to visit the Willamette Valley for wine tasting, come during harvest season, September through October.
- For outdoor activities and watersports, like kayaking, rafting, and stand-up paddleboarding, visit from June to September, when sunshine and blue skies are abundant.
- If you're on a tight budget, the best months to visit are mid-to-late September or January.

NORTHWEST OR

NW Oregon Zoom Map

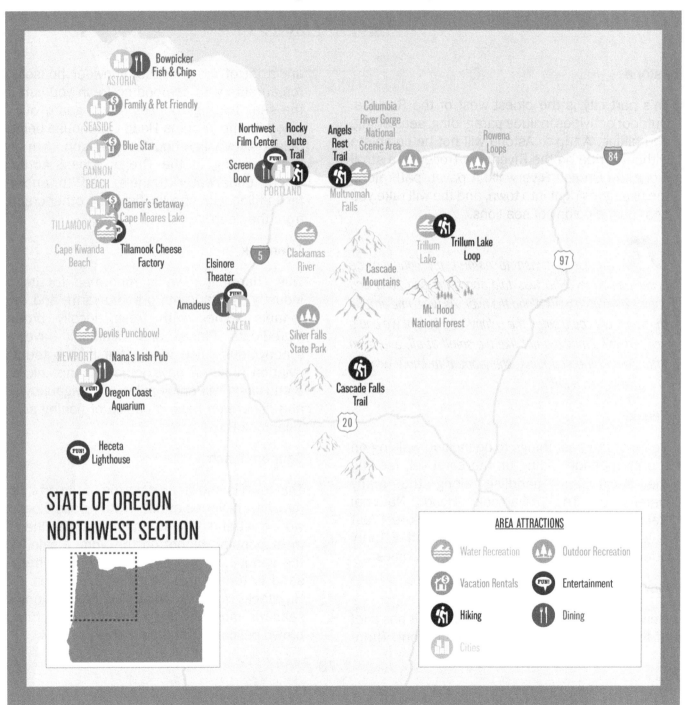

Section #1 - Northwest Oregon

Meet the Metro

Astoria

This port city is the oldest west of the Rockies. Outdoor activities include paragliding, sea fishing, and hiking. A trip to Astoria will not be complete without a ride on the Riverfront Trolley or a stroll along the Oregon Riverwalk. A paved path along the river goes right into town, and the will take you right past a colony of sea lions.

On our last visit to Astoria, my young niece accompanied us. She was told about the sea lions and could not wait to walk along the river. As we came around the bend, we could smell the colony long before we could see it. Little Emily did not like the smell at all, and even after seeing the sea lions, she wanted to know why no one gives them a bath.

Seaside

Some of the best things to do include walking on the promenade, riding on the carousel, feeding the seals, and paddling along the many waterways. The Tillamook Head National Recreation Trail runs through the rainforest just outside of town, while the Necanicum Estuary offers bird- and whale-watching opportunities.

Newport

Newport is in the big Yaquina Bay, and it has a lot of fishing boats and a working waterfront. There are a lot of art galleries, chowder houses, and restaurants with seafood so fresh you can taste the sea. Two lighthouses stand guard over the city, with the Yaquina Head Lighthouse being the tallest active lighthouse in Oregon. A must-do when visiting is the Oregon Coast Aquarium, where underwater tunnels lead to enormous tanks filled with sharks, fish, and other creatures from the deep.

Tillamook

This charming town is renowned for its dairy industry. Restaurants prepare farm- and ocean-to-table dishes with fresh, locally produced ingredients. Planes and Tillamook have been synonymous since World War II, and today the aviation museum, pays homage to this link. Water enthusiasts will enjoy miles of navigable waters, and fishermen have a choice of fishing spots in Tillamook Bay.

Cannon Beach

This town is known as a patron of the arts, as the many art galleries attest. Watch glass blowers at work or attend a theater performance. One of the most popular events on the annual calendar is the sandcastle building competition, where wet sand is turned into stunning sculptures. Iconic Haystack Rock is home to large colonies of seabirds, including the colorful Tufted Puffins and brown pelicans that feed in the surf.

Cannon Beach, Oregon

Portland

If you love the great outdoors, you will fall in love with Portland. The city is known for its many green spaces, but there is a lot more to this eclectic and vibrant city. Many of the country's top chefs call Portland home, fine dining and street food are aplenty. Booklovers will get lost in Powell's City of Books, spanning over three stories high. The city is unofficially spread across six "quadrants," each with a unique vibe and culture. A visit will not be complete without connecting to the diverse local communities.

Salem

This city is the official capital of Oregon, lies in the Willamette Valley, and offers an authentic Oregon experience. Wine, waterfalls, and plenty of outdoor adventures—you can find it all in Salem. Downtown Salem has a beautiful Riverfront Park with loads of entertainment for the whole family, from the stunning, hand-carved carousel to the children's museum and the Enchanted Forest theme park.

Salem, Oregon

This Oregon road trip was planned with a lot of expectations from my travel buddies and me. Vicki, Doris, and I had been friends for years. We finally decided to explore some of our favorite spots in Oregon. It started with the Salem Riverfront and a trip on the carousel. The intricately designed horses and murals were beautiful.

We visited the Willamette Valley Pie Company, a local favorite in Salem. There were so many varieties of pies, including classic fruit pies, cream pies, and savory pies. They also offered a tour of their pie making facility, where visitors could watch the pies being made and learn about the history of the company.

71

Vicki was thrilled with the idea of making pies, as this was her forte. She eagerly watched while secretly desiring to be right in the kitchen with the other bakers. Well, unbeknownst to her, I had pre-arranged a baking class for the three of us. We were excited to learn some new baking skills, but things did not go according to plan. Doris accidentally spilled flour all over me, then I tripped and knocked over a bowl of apples, causing Vicki to slip on a peel and land on the floor with a thud. Despite the chaos, we persevered and managed to salvage our ingredients. The pie turned out surprisingly delicious, and we could not stop laughing about our comical adventure in the kitchen.

Our next stop was Portland where we discovered the city's obsession with donuts. We tried Blue Star and Pip's Original Donuts, both famous bakeries that had lines out their doors. Doris and Vicki couldn't resist the quirky flavors, including bacon maple, grape Tang, and chocolate almond ganache. But I, at Pip's Donuts loved the "made to order mini donuts", so the guilt wasn't too bad if I ordered a dozen.

The next day we headed to the International Rose Test Garden which was in full bloom. We were mesmerized by its beautiful roses as we wandered through the rows of flowers, taking in the fragrances. Powell's City of Books was an absolute delight for us book lovers. It was like getting lost in a maze of literature!

Our final destination was Newport Beach, a coastal town known for its seafood. We could feel the cool sea breeze on our faces as we explored the historic Yaquina Bay lighthouse. Of course, we could not leave without sampling some of the local seafood specialties, like clam chowder and fish and chips. We were grateful for the sweet memories we had made together on our trip to Oregon.

Entrées and Edibles

Amadeus, Salem

This family-owned and -operated restaurant prides itself on serving contemporary American food in a cozy setting. The atmosphere is warm and friendly, along with excellent service.

Bowpicker Fish and Chips, Astoria

You'll have to travel a long way to find fresher prepared fish than at this small fast-food joint. The signature dish of beer-battered chunks of fresh albacore tuna served on a bed of thick, crunchy fries attracts visitors from across the region.

Lardo, Portland

This popular sandwich shop started out as a food cart and now has three permanent locations across Portland. The portions are enormous, and every sandwich is a unique creation.

Nana's Irish Pub, Newport

This pub honors Bridget O'Brien from Limerick City, Ireland, whose inspiration defines its food and generosity. The menu includes traditional Irish dishes like scotch eggs, and Donegal shrimp rolls. Try the traditional Irish bread pudding for dessert while listening to live Irish music.

The Screen Door, Portland

The Louisiana husband-and-wife team aim to bring the experience of southern food to the Northwest. Dishes include southern favorites like Cajun boiled peanuts and a fried chicken dinner, while desserts include Creole pecan pie and Banoffee pie.

Vacation Homes

Family and pet friendly, four-bedroom home, Seaside

Just half a block from the Seaside Promenade and beach, this is the ideal beach vacation home. The friendly open-plan living space offers the perfect spot for the family to gather after a day at the beach. The house sleeps ten people in four bedrooms, has a fully equipped kitchen and an outside propane BBQ.

Blue Star by AvantStay, Cannon Beach

This luxury two-bedroom ocean view house is available for long stays. Only a mile from Cannon Beach's quaint downtown and a short stroll to shops and restaurants, the house is centrally located. The home has spectacular ocean and Haystack views.

Garner's Getaway, Oceanside (Tillamook area)

Visitors can see Cape Lookout, Netarts Bay, and the beautiful Pacific Ocean from a wide range of angles. A quick stroll will take you to Oceanside, while the beach is just a few steps away. The Three Capes Loop offers hiking, kayaking, fishing, biking, and golfing nearby. Pets are welcome if pre-arranged.

Entertainment and Tourism

Northwest Film Center, Portland (PAM CUT)

The Northwest Film Center's vision is to encourage the study and appreciation of film as an art medium. All through the year, the center has film shows that include experimental and independent works by local artists. The Portland International Film Festival, the Northwest Filmmakers' Festival, and the Top-Down Rooftop Cinema series are all big events that happen during the year.

Oregon Coast Aquarium, Newport Beach

This isn't your average aquarium. It's an exhibition center for aquatic and marine science with a series of underwater tunnels that make it feel like you're walking under the sea. Exhibitions include sandy shores, rocky shores, and coastal waters. Visitors have panoramic views while walking through the underwater glass tunnels of the 3,000 sea creatures that form part of the exhibition.

Heceta Lighthouse, Yachats

Heceta Head is a 200-foot bluff stretching into the Pacific Ocean. On top of this dramatic rock formation stands a 56-foot-tall lighthouse that has kept ships safe since 1894. You can see the lighthouse from the tidepools and picnic tables on the beach, but to really appreciate its towering beauty, you should hike the 7-mile trail at Heceta Head Lighthouse State Scenic Viewpoint.

Other entertainment options include:

- Oregon Museum of Science and Industry, Portland
- NBA, Portland Trailblazers
- Elsinore Theatre, Salem
- St Johns Bridge, Cathedral Park, Portland

Outdoor Recreation

State Parks and Camping
Dramatic cliffs dropping into the sea, dense rainforests, and rolling meadows is **Oswald State Park in Cannon Beach**. Add to that the many species of wildlife, a beach cove, beautiful creeks, waterfalls, and you have many reasons to visit. Picnic on Short Sand Beach between the outcroppings of Smugglers Cove. The Devil's Cauldron, located high on the cliffs, is worth the quarter-mile climb, and it is an unforgettable experience to look over the cliffs that drop hundreds of feet into the sea.

Smugglers Cove, Oregon

Silver Falls State Park is the largest park in Oregon. The Silver Creek runs through the park, and its ten waterfalls gave the park its name. The most impressive of these falls is the South Falls, which cascade 177 feet into Silver Creek. The Trail of Ten Falls is a 7.4-mile loop that passes by all ten waterfalls. Apart from the hiking opportunities, the park offers a number of biking and riding trails.

Other parks in the area to visit include:

- Cape Lookout State Park, Tillamook
- Crown Point State Park, Corbett

74

- Ecola State Park, Cannon Beach
- South Beach State Park, Newport Beach

Rowena Loops, Mosier Oregon

National Parks, Forests and Monuments

Right in **Mount Hood National Forest**, Mount Hood towers above the Oregon landscape like an icy pyramid. This mountain stands 11,245 feet tall and is the fourth highest peak in the Cascade Range. Take a leisurely stroll down the Trillium Lake Loop Trail; it is an easy route, popular for fishing, hiking, and mountain biking. During the winter, sports like mushing, skiing, snowboarding, sledding, and snowshoeing are popular and attract visitors from across the region.

Columbia River Gorge National Scenic Area has a spectacular river canyon that meanders for 80 miles through the Cascade Range. Easy walks will take you past the Rowena Crest and its wildflowers, or you can trek up Dog Mountain for a more strenuous workout. The Columbia River offers many water sports in the warmer months.

The Rowena Loops is a section of the Mosier Oregon Road that is located in the Columbia River Gorge. The section of road is known for its hairpin turns, which provide breathtaking views at every angle. The Rowena Loops is a popular destination for cyclists, as it offers a challenging and scenic ride through the Columbia River Gorge.

A famous park in the area you may want to visit is the **Lewis and Clark National Historical Park** near Astoria. The park is situated on the banks of the Sandy River, offering hiking trails, camping sites and picnic areas. Visitors can also go fishing, boating, and swimming in the river.

Treks

The Rocky Butte Trail is relatively steep in some sections, but there are also some flat areas along the way.
Stats: 2.6 miles out and back, moderate

Angel's Rest Trail is known for its stunning views of the Columbia River Gorge and the surrounding mountains. The trail gains about 1,500 feet in elevation and offers panoramic views of the Gorge. On a clear day, visitors can see as far as Mount Hood and Mount St. Helens.
Stats: 4.5 miles out and back, challenging

Other treks in the region include:

- Warrior Rock Lighthouse Point Trailhead, Warren, 1.5 miles, easy
- Wildwood Newberry Trailhead, Portland, 3.7 miles, moderate
- Cascade Falls Trail, 2.4 miles, moderate
- Trillium Lake Loop, 2 miles, easy
- McNeil Point Trail, 9 miles, difficult
- Tamanawas Falls Trail, 3.6 miles, moderate
- Mark O Hatfield E Trail, 7.3 miles, easy to moderate

Bald Mountain Trail, Oregon

Water Recreation

Windsurfing

Hood River Oregon is located on the Columbia River Gorge and known as the windsurfing capital of the world. The river is wide enough to provide ample room for windsurfers; an ideal location for beginners to learn and for advanced windsurfers to perfect their skills. The region is a picturesque canyon that is narrow in width and consistently experiences strong winds.

Other windsurfing sites are:

- The Oregon Coast: Pistol River, Gold Beach, and Lincoln City
- The Gorge Windsurfing Park
- Detroit Lake
- The Deschutes River
- Floras Lake located in Southern Oregon

The competitive sister duo, Monette and Andi set out on their windsurfing adventure with excitement. The wind was perfect, and the waves were just right for some thrilling action. As they sailed side by side, Monette decided to show off her skills and performed a daring jump, only to lose her balance by falling into the water with a loud splash. Andi laughed hysterically as she helped her sister back onto her board. Then, Monette challenged Andi to a race back to the pier. As they pushed forward, Andi and Monette felt the speed coursing through their bodies. Suddenly, a large wave lifted Andi up and for a brief moment, she was airborne. Andi landed back on the board with a splash and rode the waves until she cruised by Monette, feeling a sense of exhilaration. The two continued surfing, their laughter echoing across the water. Another exhilarating day!

Lakes

Cape Meares Lake, also known as "Bayocean Lake," this is a man-made, freshwater lake situated on the southern end of the Bayocean Peninsula Park. At the lake, visitors can enjoy hiking, swimming, kayaking, and canoeing. A great spot for fishing for largemouth bass, and rainbow trout.

Other popular lakes in the region are:

- Timothy Lake, Mount Hood
- Sturgeon Lake, Sauvie Island
- Trillium Lake, Mount Hood

Trillium Lake, Mount Hood, Oregon

Rivers

The **Clackamas River** is known for its stunning natural beauty with plush forests, sparkling waters, and rocky cliffs. The river winds through the Cascade mountains and is a common destination for fishing, kayaking, rafting, swimming, and hiking.

Jerry and his fishing buddy Will were out on the Clackamas River for a day of fishing. They decided to have a friendly competition to see who could catch the most fish. As they were fishing, they noticed that the river had a strong current and was quite deep in some areas. Jerry joked that if he fell in, he'd need a snorkel to breathe. Will laughed and said he'd need a life jacket. Jerry suddenly felt a tug on his line. He started reeling in the fish, but as it got closer, he realized that it was not a fish at all. It was a pair of underwear! Will couldn't stop laughing as Jerry held up the underwear.

More rivers in the region are:

- Willamette River
- Yachats River
- Columbia River
- Nehalem River
- Sandy River

Waterfalls

To get to **House Rock Falls** in Foster, hike a short loop through the rainforest to the viewpoint. The falls drop about 60 feet into a pool surrounded by greenery. During the rainy season, the waterfall thunders across large mossy boulders, but by the end of summer, the water subsides to a small stream.

It is known as the most popular waterfall in the Pacific Northwest. The two, two-tiered falls is easily accessible on foot and will take you right up to the base of the 611-foot-tall roaring falls. The upper falls are the fifth highest waterfall in the United States and the lower falls are the second highest. The Multnomah Falls Lodge has a restaurant, gift shop, and great views of the falls.

Multnomah Falls, Oregon

Tamolitch Falls in Willamette, otherwise known as the "Blue Pool" is a basin surrounded by cliffs and a popular spot for visitors. The falls only flow in spring, yet the pool is continuously fed by underground springs.

Dropping about 70 feet into a pool below is the **Fall Creek Falls** in the Willamette National Forest.

The trail is open to hiking, horseback riding, mountain biking and has several campgrounds.

More waterfalls to visit:

- Latourell Falls Loop Trail, Corbet
- South Falls, Salem
- Triple Falls, Columbia River gorge
- Abiqua Falls near Salem

Beaches

The **Devils Punchbowl State Beach** is named after a sea cave whose ceiling collapsed many years ago, leaving the "bowl" open to the sky. The waves rushing in and thundering against the crater walls live up to the dramatic name given to the cave. The area is rich in marine wildlife, and whales may be spotted feeding in the kelp beds.

Cape Kiwanda Beach, Pacific City is a sandy beach known as one of the best places to surf in the area. People who like hang gliding, hiking, and other water sports also come here. One of the attractions is the Great Dune, standing 250 feet tall and offering views across the bay. The windy conditions are also ideal for kite flying.

Other beaches in the area are:

- Nye Beach
- Short Beach, Oceanside
- Rockaway Beach
- Cannon Beach

NORTHEAST OR

NE Oregon Zoom Map

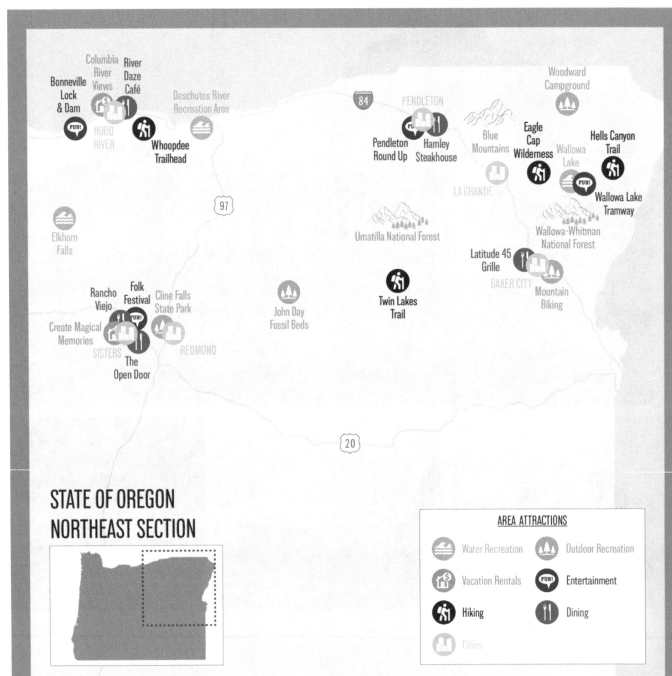

Section #2 - Northeast Oregon

Meet the Metro

Hood River

Located on the banks of the Columbus River Gorge with Mount Hood as a backdrop, this city has it all. In summer, hiking, rafting, and windsurfing are popular pastimes. While winter brings snow sports like snowboarding and skiing. The fertile soil of the area means fruit is in abundance, and when you visit, you will be spoiled by the selection of art, culture, and culinary delights.

Pendleton

Pendleton was named one of the Top ten Western Towns in the United States in 2021 (Corbett, 2021). In western tradition, the town is known for rodeos and fine leather craftsmanship. Western events take place throughout the year, with the legendary Pendleton Roundup a high point on the rodeo calendar. If you are visiting with your family, the kids will enjoy the ice rink and aquatic center.

Sisters

Visit this charming town of Sisters in central Oregon. In summer, the outdoors call for biking, hiking, and rafting. Fall is the best time to fish for trout and kokanee in one of the many lakes nearby. With winter comes snow and skiing, snowboarding, and snowshoeing. The kids will love the trampoline parks, ice skating, and activity centers. For outdoor fun, explore the Redmond Caves or visit the alpacas at Crescent Moon Ranch.

Sisters, Oregon

Redmond

One of the top attractions in Redmond is Smith Rock State Park. Considered the birthplace of rock climbing in the US, it is still one of the greatest places to climb. Bring your camera along and capture the rock spires or the sheer cliffs leading down into the river canyon. A visit to Steelhead Falls is a must; a short hike takes you to the beautiful falls with several swimming holes. Bring a picnic and spend the day!

La Grande

Home to Eastern Oregon University, nestled between the Blue and Wallowa Mountain ranges, the scenery is beautiful. The city is the ideal base camp for visits to Blue Mountain, Anthony Lakes, and Hells Canyon National Recreation Area. For the more culturally minded, the Grande Ronde Symphony Orchestra has symphonic concerts year-round.

Baker City

The town of Baker City is home to more than 100 historic buildings. The downtown district offers art galleries, wine shops, and many eateries in some of its beautiful buildings. For even more history, explore the Oregon Trail, visit historic sites, and camp next to ancient lakes. People will be amazed by how the old and the new things coexist in this town.

Entrées and Edibles

Latitude 45 Grille, Baker City

This family-friendly restaurant is in the historic Antlers Hotel, just off Main Street. It serves a wide range of foods; their baby back ribs come highly recommended! Dine indoors or sit outside when the weather permits and watch the world go by.

Rancho Viejo, Sisters

This Mexican restaurant is one of the best-known Mexican restaurants in central Oregon, and once you have tasted the authentic cuisine, you will understand why. Mexican favorites are made from scratch using authentic Mexican recipes.

Hamley Steakhouse and Saloon, Pendleton

The old western-style saloon offers a menu fit for any cowboy. The California Cowgirl Burger will satisfy even the hungriest cowgirl in the region. Take a walk through the western store and visit the second floor where local and national artists sell their work.

River Daze Café, Hood River

The restaurant offers quality, handcrafted food made from local ingredients. Their specialty sandwiches are made on-site with freshly baked bread. Also on offer are organic soups and kombucha, as well as a variety of local microbrews.

The Open Door, Sisters

Guests are made to feel welcome in this cozy restaurant. Delicious, wholesome food served with some of the best local wines makes the menu a winner. The homemade coconut pie is a favorite. In the warm months, enjoy outside seating under the tall pine trees.

Vacation Homes

Create Magical Memories, Sisters

Pine Meadow Village, where this well-equipped condo is, has a clubhouse, a swimming pool, tennis courts, and paved walking paths. Sisters' downtown is just a few minutes' walk away. The west-facing patio and living room offer views of five beautiful mountains.

Downtown with Columbia River views, Hood River

This long-term residence is conveniently located, and a short walk will take you to the heart of downtown to Hood River's restaurants and coffee shops. The house is situated a mere five-minute drive from the river and all the water sports it offers.

Entertainment and Tourism

Folk Festival, Sisters

The event features more than 30 artists performing in seven venues and takes place in the last week of September. The whole town of Sisters joins in to create a week filled with folk music.

Lock and Dam Visitor Center, Bonneville

The Bonneville Dam is a well-known landmark in the area. It is in the Columbia River Gorge. The dam has one of the largest hydroelectric systems in the world. The Bradford Island Visitor Center has exhibits about the construction of the dam, the history of the area, and information on the salmon that breed in the water. Visitors can view a "fish ladder" from the rooftop observation deck.

Hood River BIG ART Walking Tour, Hood River

This 4.5-mile hike on the banks of the Hood River leads through parks and businesses where a collection of sculptures can be seen. While the artwork is for visual enjoyment, there is one piece that is designed to move and interact with the viewer. "House with Round Windows" plays with wind and light to give an immersive experience.

Pendleton Roundup

Pendleton Round Up is a legendary rodeo event held annually in Oregon. It features thrilling competition, including bull riding and barrel racing as well as concerts and parades. Attending the Round Up offers a unique opportunity to experience Western culture, witness impressive horsemanship skills and indulge in delicious food.

Willowa Lake Tramway

Experience the Willowa Lake Tramway in Joseph, Oregon and enjoy breathtaking views of the neighboring Mountains. The tramway offers several attractions and activities. At the top visitors can explore the observation deck with additional panoramic sights.

Mountain Biking, Baker City

From rolling mountainside to high alpine terrain, summer mountain biking trails are transformed into winter ski slopes. This area between LaGrande and Baker City is known as a premier mountain biking region. One family-friendly ride is the 15-mile Phillips Lake Loop in the Elkhorn Mountains. Experienced riders can take on the

Black Butte, Sisters, Oregon

Lookout Mountain Loop, which has been called one of the best downhill trails in Central Oregon.

Outdoor Recreation

National Forests

The **Umatilla National Forest**, at 1.4 million acres, is home to one of the largest herds of Rocky Mountain elk in the country. Other animals found are mule deer, whitetail deer, and bighorn sheep. The forest offers more than 715 miles of trails and around 20 campgrounds throughout the forest.

If you are looking to camp, try the **Woodward Campground near Tollgate**. The campground is in the shade of trees and is on the edge of a private lake, Langdon Lake.

Other campgrounds in the area include:

- LaGrande Rendezvous RV Park
- Umatilla Forks Campground

Treks

- Grouse Mountain Trail, 5.2 miles, moderate
- Umatilla Rim Trail, 8.5 miles, moderate

Wallowa-Whitman National Forest

With scenic vistas, high mountain lakes, and rocky ridges, this forest's diverse landscape is a must to experience. The secluded **Boulder Creek Campground** near Cornucopia is a favorite with visitors. The camp has only seven tent spots and

is located on the South Umpqua River under a canopy of trees.

Other camping sites include:

- Two Color Guard Station Campground, Medical Springs
- Catherine Creek Campground, Telocaset

Treks

The **Twin Lakes Trail** starts near Frog Lake Sno-Park and is a loop of moderate difficulty over 7 miles. A trek suitable for experienced hikers is the Chief Joseph Mountain Trail. The hike is 7 miles one way, and there are fishing opportunities.

Other hikes in the area:

- Hoffer Lakes Trail, 7.6 miles, moderate
- Lakes Basin Trails:
    - Ice Lake Trail, 8.4 miles, moderate
    - Aneroid Lake Trail, 12 miles, moderate
    - Horseshoe Lake Trail, 6 miles, easy
    - Mirror Lake Trail, 3 miles, easy
- Eagle Cap Wilderness Trail, 26 miles, difficult
- Hells Canyon Trail, 26 miles, difficult
- Wallowa Lake Trail, 3.5 miles, easy

State Parks and Camping

Smith Park State Park is located in the high desert of Oregon, the park is situated on rocky ground and surrounded by towering rock faces.

The park has an extensive network of trails with views of the river canyons and steep cliffs. They offer some of the best rock climbing in the region, while hikers and mountain bikers are also blessed for opportunity.

Cline Falls State Park is located along the Deschutes River in central Oregon. The falls is the main attraction to the park and has a viewpoint showing the 10 feet water drop over a rocky ledge surrounded by beautiful scenery.

Other state parks worth a visit:

- Wallowa Lake State Park
- Emigrant Springs State Park
- Hat Rock State Park
- Ukiah Dale Forest State Scenic Corridor
- Catherine Creek State Park

Treks

There are plenty of activities to do in the **Blue Mountains** of Oregon. Hiking trails are plentiful, with varying difficulty levels. The mountain range offers abundant fishing options with its many streams and lakes. For the adventurous, mountain biking provides exciting descents and challenging climbs. Don't miss out on a trek on what is considered one of the most scenic trails of the Pacific Northwest, the **Elkhorn Crest Trail**.

The **John Day Fossil Beds National Monument** offers a variety of hiking trails that are generally considered easy to moderate.

- Painted Hills Unit
    - Painted Cover Trail, .25 miles, easy
    - Leaf Hill Trail, 1 mile, easy

- Painted Hills Overlook Trail, 1.5 miles, moderate
- Carroll Rim Trail, 1.6 miles, moderate
- Red Hill Trail, 3 miles, moderate

The sun slowly rose over the Painted Hills of the John Day Fossil Beds National Monument. We were excited to share this natural wonder with our children. We hiked trails together as their eyes widened with wonder. They took in the vibrant patterns and colors of red, gold,

and green layers around them. My daughter giggled as she found a small rock shaped like a heart and my son eagerly pointed out the different layers of sediment. We paused, lost in God's wonderous creation.

- Sheep Rock Unit
    - Blue Basis Overlook Trail, 1.3 miles, easy
    - Island in Time Trail, 1.3 miles, easy
    - Story in Stone Trail, 0.3 miles, easy
    - Flood of Fire Trail, 1.5 miles, moderate

- Clarno Unit
  - Clarno Arch Trail, 1.4 miles, easy
  - Geologic Time Trail, 2.2 miles, moderate

Eagle Cap Wilderness is home to a diverse range of landscapes, including snowcapped peaks, deep valleys, alpine meadows, and dense forests. One popular trail is the **Lakes Basin Loop**.
Stats: 20 miles, difficult

Redmond Caves Recreation owns a unique geological formation in its land. Caves have been formed by lava tubes. Visitors can explore them by crawling or hiking through the underground tunnels. The area is home to several species of bats, and they can be seen in the summer months in the caves roosting in their natural habitat.
Stats: 2.2 miles, easy

Other hiking trails to explore are:

- Catherine Creek Trail, 3.3 miles, easy
- Joseph Canyon Trail, 12 miles, moderate
- Mount Ruth Trail, 8 miles, difficult

Water Recreation

Lakes

Wallowa Lake is a family friendly lake. Enjoy a tram ride to the top of Mount Howard with scenic views over the alpine wilderness and surrounding mountains. Play miniature golf or ride on the bumper boat. There are more than 500 miles of developed trails, so bring your hiking boots along!

Other lakes in the area include:

- Lake Billy Chinook
- Detroit Lake
- Green Peter Lake

Waterfalls

Elkhorn Falls is a 50-foot waterfall located in the Elkhorn Mountains near the town of Baker City. The falls are accessible via a short hike and offer fabulous views of the surrounding wilderness. Visitors can also explore the nearby Elkhorn Creek to enjoy fishing and swimming in the area.

Other waterfalls in the area are:

- South Fork Falls
- Imnaha Falls
- White River Falls
- Wallowa Falls

Rivers

Leisurely float down the **Deschutes River** located in the Deschutes River State Recreation Park next to the pavilion. Choose between a one- or two-hour float before returning in the Ride the River Shuttle. Lower in the river, the rapids become more intense, and whitewater rafting provides hours of fun. Bring your fishing tackle and fish for trout or steelhead. Or just hike along one of the gentle trails and take in the surrounding beauty.

Other rivers in the area are:

- North Powder River
- Malheur River, Prairie City
- Imnaha River

SOUTHWEST OR

SW Oregon Zoom Map

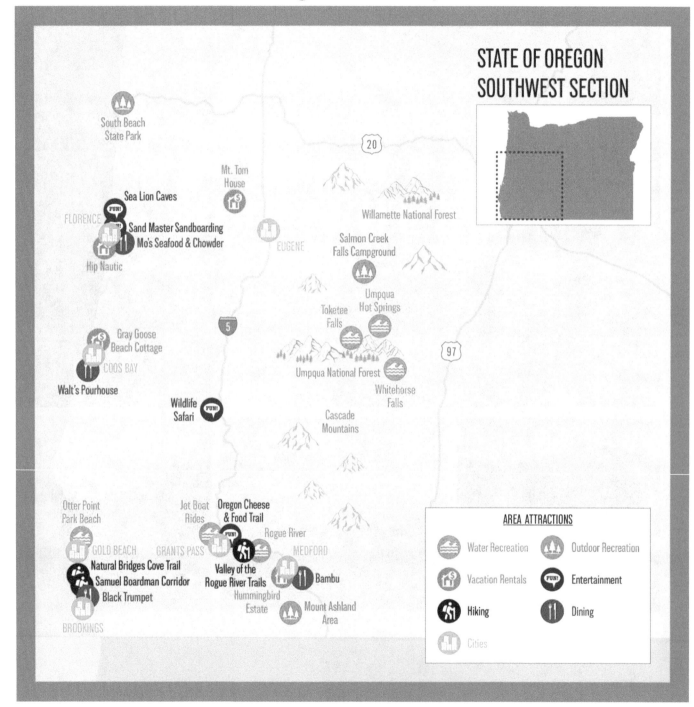

Section #3 - Southwest Oregon

Meet the Metro

Florence

Florence Bridge, Oregon

If you are looking for a seaside experience, this charming town offers beaches with rolling dunes. The historic old town of Florence is a great place for art lovers. The famous sand dunes offer dune buggy tours or sandboarding. If you visit during the summer months, you will be able to watch the whales as they migrate to the waters of Mexico.

Coos Bay

This port city has a very active working harbor. Coos Bay is a favorite spot for storm watching, with swells up to 20 feet creating gigantic waves that thunder and break on the bluff. The Southern Oregon Coastal Wilderness, with its sandy beaches and wildlife-filled forests, is only a short drive from the city. Coos Bay is host to several events throughout the year.

Gold Beach

If you are looking for a laid-back holiday, this quiet town is a good choice. The Wild Rivers Coast Scenic Bikeway is a scenic ride next to the ocean leading past cranberry bogs and towering sea stacks. This untouched area is a birdwatcher's dream because there are so many places for birds to live. Gold Beach and its environments are well-known for year-round fishing in nearby rivers and the ocean.

Eugene

Eugene is home to TrackTown USA. The University of Oregon brings youth and life to a city rich in culture and innovation. Downtown offers many fantastic boutique shops, art galleries, and eateries. The flourishing markets include art activities and musical entertainment, making it an ideal family outing. Nature is at the city's doorstep offering many hiking, biking, water sports, and fishing opportunities.

Grants Pass

The city lies on the banks of the Rogue River, and it is a great base for exciting outdoor adventures. The city is home to beautiful parks like Riverside Park, where there is plenty of opportunity to feed the birds that frequent the park or walk through All Sports Park while strolling over its many bridges. The river provides plenty of opportunities for water sports, and river rafting is very popular.

Entrées and Edibles

Mo's Seafood and Chowder, Florence

This seafood restaurant has been family-owned and operated for over 70 years. The clam chowder is so popular that the base is sold in local shops to make at home. Fish in all shapes and forms can be ordered here, from halibut to Alaskan cod or Yaquina Bay oysters.

Walt's Pourhouse, Coos Bay

Walt's Pourhouse is a sports bar with 16 beers on tap and classic bar games like pool and shuffleboard. The large menu offers vegetarian meals to chowder and burgers.

Bambu, Medford

The far east has come to Medford with a menu that offers regional cuisine from countries like Japan, China, and the Philippines.

Black Trumpet Bistro, Brookings

Black Trumpet Bistro is a cozy restaurant known for creative and seasonal cuisine. The menu features a variety of dishes made with fresh, locally sourced ingredients. It is known for traditionally inspired dishes with a modern twist.

Vacation Homes

Gray Goose Beach Cottage, Coos Bay

This charming coastal retreat cottage is right on the water and offers direct access to the bay shore. Relish the beautiful scenery and the perfect location.

Hip Nautic, Florence

A modern home near the beach. It is located just five miles north of Florence's shops and restaurants with easy access to explore the Oregon coastline

Mount Tom House, Harrisburg

Mount Tom House is a charming property nestled in the Coburg Hills. It has six beautiful bedrooms, and rooms can be booked separately, or you can book the whole house for a family gathering. A full breakfast is served in the historic dining room each morning for guests to enjoy. There are 120 miles of hiking trails near the house, which is in a nature preserve.

Hummingbird Estate, Medford

The Hummingbird Estate is a working wine farm. During the year, the estate hosts a number of events, such as live music by a number of local artists. There are five rooms in the main house. Breakfast and a wine tasting are included.

Entertainment and Tourism

Oregon Cheese and Food Trail

You may not know that Oregon is famous for artisan cheese and even has an annual cheese festival held at the Rogue Creamery. There are classes and tastings with talks about the 250 kinds of cow, sheep, and goat cheese made in the area. Plan a road trip around cheese and visit creameries in lush green valleys and in seaside mountain towns across the state.

![binoculars icon] *The Oregon Cheese and Food Trail promised adventure and excitement which did not disappoint. As Tracy and Debra set out on their journey, they encountered a group of dairy cows, who seemed to be staring at them with intense curiosity. Tracy couldn't help but laugh as they followed them both with their big brown eyes. Their first stop was the Rogue Creamery, where they tasted some of the most delicious cheese they'd ever had. Next, they headed to the Blue Heron French Cheese Company, where they indulged in a picnic of cheese, crackers, and fresh bread. As Tracy savored the flavors, she noticed a group of chickens clucking around, hoping for a taste of her food. They continued to the Tillamook Cheese Factory, where they viewed giant vats that mix curds and whey. Debra was amazed at how quickly the mixture transformed into cheese. They were invited to put on gloves and shape the cheese into blocks. It was an experience not to be forgotten!*

Jet Boat Rides, Grants Pass

Adrenaline junkies from all over the world come to experience the wild Rogue River on board a jet boat. This thrilling adventure combines the excitement of high-speed travel with the beauty of the natural environment. The boats are designed to handle the rapids and twists of the river, providing an exhilarating experience for all riders.

Sea Lion Caves, Florence

These fascinating caves are over twelve stories high and in places as wide as a football field. The Steller sea lions and their cubs call this home. They are often found somewhere on the property interacting in their natural habitat.

Sand Master Park, Florence

The high sand dunes found here lend themselves to sandboarding. There are acres of sand dunes that are good for beginners, as well as more difficult dunes for more experienced riders. Visitors can rent sandboards and book lessons with an expert. The annual Sand Master Jam brings together sandboarders and other outdoor fanatics from around the world.

Pear Blossom Festival, Medford

The festival started in 1954 as a children's parade, but soon it bloomed into the extravaganza we know today. There are around 150 floats entering the parade annually and more than 5,000 participants. The festival is also host to a baby contest, several pageants, and a street fair.

Wildlife Safari, Winston

This animal park features more than 600 animals from around the world. The park offers an African safari, bringing visitors close to animals like ostriches, lions, zebras, hippos, rhinos, and even elephants. The carnivore loop has a place where endangered cheetahs and dangerous Sumatran tigers can breed. Every day, you can meet different animals at the park; you can feed red pandas and take a picture with a cheetah.

Other entertainment options include:

- Cascade Raptor Centre, Eugene
- Covered Bridges Tour, Eugene
- Bohemia Gold Mining Museum, Cottage Grove
- Prehistoric Gardens, Gold Beach,
- Sunriver Music Festival, Sunriver

Outdoor Recreation

National Forest

Umpqua National Forest

The **Acker Rock Lookout** sits on top of a rocky cliff in the Umpqua National Forest and offers visitors a unique experience. On a clear day, the mountains on the Willamette River are visible. The rock on which the lookout building sits has sheer cliffs on two sides. Visitors need to carry their bags up a steep 400-meter forest hike before reaching the building.

Bogus Creek Campground is a tranquil getaway surrounded by tall Douglas fir trees. The campground sits next to a bubbling creek that provides a soothing soundtrack to the wilderness experience. Hiking trails lead to panoramic vistas and waterfalls.

Other campgrounds in the vicinity include:

- Eagle Rock Campground
- Horseshoe Bend Campground
- Umpqua's Last Resort, Steamboat

Treks

- Trestle Creek Loop, 3.8 miles, easy to moderate
- Umpqua Hot Springs, 1.2 miles, moderate

Willamette National Forest

There are plenty of camping opportunities in the Willamette National Forest. People can also choose to camp in areas of the forest that are not set up as campgrounds. This is called "dispersed camping," and it is allowed in some parts of the forest.

Salmon Creek Falls Campground is set in a beautiful, forested area near Salmon Creek Falls. The campground is surrounded by trees and is a peaceful quiet place to relax.

Other campgrounds in the area are:

- Waldo Lake Islet Campground
- Mona Campground
- Paradise Campground

Treks

- Natural Bridges Cove Trail, 0.3 miles, easy
- Oregon Caves National Monument, 1.2 miles, easy route
- Samuel Boardman Scenic Corridor, 1.6 miles, a moderate

State Parks and Camping

South Beach State Park offers around 322 campsites, 60 tent-only sites, and 27 rustic yurts along the beautiful Oregon coastline. There are also three group tent camping areas. All the spots have electricity and water, as well as a table, fire ring, and grate. The beach and numerous hiking trails are easily accessible from the campground. There are many outdoor activities like fishing, boating, crabbing, swimming, and kayaking.

Other parks in the vicinity include:

- Elijah Bristow State Park
- Valley of the Rogue State Park
- Carl G. Washburne Memorial State Park

Treks

- Mount Ashland Recreation Area, 5.2 miles, difficult
- Devils Peak, 12 miles, difficult
- Cleetwood Cove Trail, 2 miles, moderate
- Hobart Bluff, 2.5 miles, moderate
- Puck Lake Trail, 4.5 miles, easy
- Mount Scott Trail, 4.2 miles, difficult

Samuel H Boardman, Oregon

Water Recreation

Rivers

The Rogue River, a 215-mile-long river, flows from the Cascade Range to the Pacific Ocean. It is famous for the salmon runs and the rough landscapes it passes through. There are several whitewater runs on the river, ranging in difficulty. The river is also popular with kayakers for the class 3 rapids, which are separated by gentle stretches of water and scenic deep pools.

Other rivers in the area include:

- Umpqua River
- Coos River
- Smith River
- Elk River

Waterfalls

The **Whitehorse Falls** is a small waterfall that does not attract many visitors, but it is beautiful! This hidden gem's water has a bluish tone and is pristine. There is a platform for easy access, and as it is only a short hike from the parking lot, it is family friendly.

Toketee Falls located in the Umpqua National Forest drops about 120 feet in two tiers and the water flows through a narrow chasm before plunging into a pool at the bottom. The name Toketee means "graceful" or "pretty" in the language of the Native American tribes who originally inhabited the area.

Other waterfalls in the area include:

- Barr Creek Falls
- Mill Creek Falls/Prospect State Scenic Viewpoint
- Chocolate Falls

Beaches

Florence, on the Oregon coast, has many scenic beaches to explore. Heceta Head is only 15 minutes north of the city. The beach is wind-protected and situated just below the Heceta Head Lighthouse. The beach has stunning rock formations and a few sea caves on the north end.

Bay Point Landing Beach is situated in a spectacular location surrounded by abundant forests and ocean views. The area is home to a diverse range of sea life and animals of that region, including sea lions, seals, bald eagles and more. The beach itself is pristine.

Ginny and her friends had been planning a vacation to Bay Point Landing Beach for weeks. Straight away they took advantage of biking trails to explore the Cape Arago Loop. They spotted sea lions and seals lounging on the rocks, and even caught a glimpse of bald eagles soaring overhead. Later in the day, the group decided to take a coastal tour in kayaks and noticed several seals swimming nearby, popping their heads up out of the water to watch the kayakers. Ginny, feeling adventurous, decided to get a closer look at the seals. She paddled over to where they were and started taking pictures. Suddenly, one of the seals swam right up to her kayak and started barking loudly. Ginny was startled, but she quickly realized that the seal was just trying to communicate with her. The seal continued to swim alongside her kayak, barking and splashing water with its flippers. Ginny started to laugh and paddle away, but the seal would not let her go. It kept following her as it if wanted to play. Her friends watched in amazement as Ginny and the seal continued their game of cat-and-mouse. They couldn't stop laughing as they watched the seal chase after Ginny's kayak, trying to get her attention. Finally, after several minutes, the seal grew tired and swam away. Ginny and her friends continued their kayaking adventure, but they all agreed that the highlight of the trip was the hilarious encounter with the friendly seal.

Other beaches in the area include:

- Otter Point Park Beach
- Oregon Dunes Beach
- Bullard's Beach
- Bandon Beach

SOUTHEAST OR

SE Oregon Zoom Map

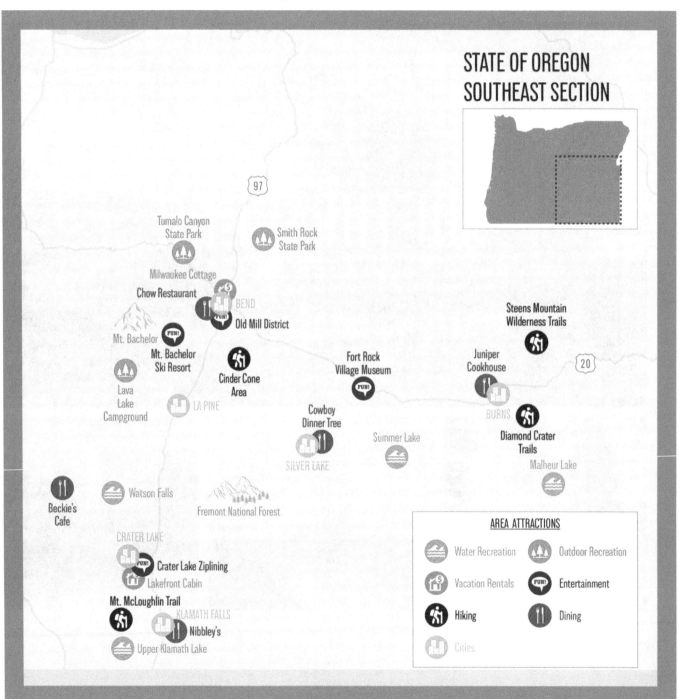

STATE OF OREGON
SOUTHEAST SECTION

Tumalo Canyon State Park

Smith Rock State Park

Milwaukee Cottage

Chow Restaurant

BEND

Old Mill District

Mt. Bachelor

Mt. Bachelor Ski Resort

Cinder Cone Area

Steens Mountain Wilderness Trails

Fort Rock Village Museum

Juniper Cookhouse

Lava Lake Campground

LA PINE

Cowboy Dinner Tree

Summer Lake

BURNS

Diamond Crater Trails

SILVER LAKE

Malheur Lake

Beckie's Cafe

Watson Falls

Fremont National Forest

CRATER LAKE

Crater Lake Ziplining

Lakefront Cabin

Mt. McLoughlin Trail

KLAMATH FALLS

Nibbley's

Upper Klamath Lake

AREA ATTRACTIONS

Water Recreation · Outdoor Recreation
Vacation Rentals · Entertainment
Hiking · Dining
Cities

Section #4 - Southeast Oregon

Meet the Metro

Bend

The Deschutes River flows through the city, creating many opportunities for water sports. It is no wonder Bend is home to the first urban whitewater park in the state. Take a stroll through one of the city's 80 parks. In winter, sports like skiing, snowboarding, snowshoeing, and ice skating are popular pastimes. Bend has a vibrant culinary scene, and foodies from around the world visit for a taste of what the city can offer.

La Pine

The city is located in the valley of the Little Deschutes River, with the Cascade Mountains in the background. The city was named for the majestic pine trees in the area. There are many things to do at the Newberry National Volcanic Monument that are related to the volcanoes in the area. For a unique experience, check out the spooky Lava Cave Forest or the Lava River Cave.

Burns

Ranching, sheep farming, logging, and tourism drive the local economy. One of the big attractions is the Crystal Crane Hot Springs. Burns is wild horse country. Keep your eyes and ears open; you may be lucky enough to come upon a herd in your travels. The Malheur National Wildlife Refuge is home to more than 300 different kinds of birds, perfect for bird watching experiences.

Crater Lake

Crater Lake is the deepest lake in America, and scientists believe the lake is the result of a volcanic event many years ago. The lake is in Oregon's only national park and is known to get some of the heaviest snowfall in the country. In the park, you can stay at the Crater Lake Lodge, the Cabins at Mazama Village, or the Mazama Campground.

Mountain Fall Colors in Bend and Crater Lake, Oregon

Klamath Falls

Klamath Falls is nicknamed "Oregon's City of Sunshine", and one of the best ways to discover what the town can offer is to take a self-guided stroll. Birdwatchers love the town because the National Wildlife Refuge Complex is home to over 350 species of birds, making it one of the

97

most important birding areas in North America. Klamath Falls has great restaurants, a lively performance scene, and beautiful scenery. In the winter, make time to look for bald eagles, which can be found in large numbers in the area.

Entrées and Edibles

The McKay's Cottage, Bend

Indulge at McKay's Cottage, Bend's Culinary Gem! Savor exquisite farm-to-table delights, from heavenly cinnamon-spiced pancakes to mouthwatering bacon-wrapped dates. Visit McKay's Cottage and discover why it is one of Bend's favorite food havens!

Cowboy Dinner Tree, Silver Lake

Years ago, the restaurant began as a lunch stop for local ranchers beneath a juniper tree. Today, this is still a rustic restaurant serving good old-fashioned cowboy fare. Book a cabin and stay over after dinner and remember to visit the gift shop for western artistries before you head home.

The Cowboy Dinner Tree was known for its huge portions of food including steaks and chicken and homemade bread. Melissa and her husband, Greg, had heard about it and decided to try it out for dinner. They were greeted by friendly staff who seated them at a cozy table. The menu was simple: steak or chicken, served with all the trimmings. Greg and Melissa opted for the steak and were stunned when it arrived, sizzling on a hot plate, accompanied by a generous helping of mashed potatoes and vegetables. They barely made a dent in the massive

portion but couldn't resist trying the homemade pie for dessert. As they savored each bite, they shared stories and laughed, creating a delightful evening together.

Nibbley's, Klamath Falls

At Nibbley's, the philosophy is that customers should leave eager to come back. The restaurant has a beautiful main area and a relaxed outdoor patio where delicious food can be enjoyed. The restaurant has received numerous awards for excellence in food and service.

Juniper Cookhouse, Burns

If baked goods are your passion, be sure to visit the rustic Juniper Cookhouse. Pies, cheesecakes, and cookies are made to order or can be enjoyed on a picnic table under the pine trees. The restaurant is also known for its mouthwatering steaks and hamburgers, made from locally sourced, grass-fed beef.

Vacation Homes

Secluded Lakefront Cabin, Crater Lake

The lakefront cabin has direct access to a privately owned reservoir. The water is teeming with largemouth bass, and guests are able to fish for their own dinner. The cabin has a deck with beautiful views of the water and forest.

Milwaukee, a Cheerful Cottage, Bend

The cottage is in the middle of town, on the west side. Restaurants, coffee bars, and other entertainment are within walking distance.

Entertainment and Tourism

Mount Bachelor Ski Resort

This resort is a mere 30-minute drive from downtown Bend and is the 6th largest resort in North America. With more than 4,300 skiable acres and 121 unique runs, this is a must-do if you are into winter sports. For a magical experience, book a ride on a dog sled team led by a professional musher along the tree-lined trails of Mount Bachelor. Regular snowshoe tours depart from the resort. Snowshoes are provided, and no experience is needed; a ranger will lead the hike.

Klamath Folk Alliance Showcase Series

The Klamath Folk Festival is a collaboration between the Klamath Folk Alliance and the Ross Ragland Theater to give local talent the chance to perform on stage. There are numerous performances during the festival. Some of the talented musicians discovered here have gone unsigned with music labels; an example is The Brothers Reed, who have released their fifth studio album recently. Apart from the festival itself, the Showcase Series has local artists performing throughout the year.

Crater Lake Zipline, Klamath Falls

In the mood for a different kind of outdoor fun? A zipline canopy tour with stunning views of the Cascade Mountains may be in the cards. It boasts of nine ziplines and two suspended bridges, which are sure to get the adrenaline pumping. Experienced guides make sure that even the most inexperienced zipliners have a fun-filled day. There is the option to combine ziplining and kayaking for even more amusement or try your hand at axe-throwing at the axe-throwing range. If you need sustenance after all the excitement, visit Sassy's kitchen for delicious food and something cold to drink.

Fort Rock Village Museum

Is a must visit attraction that offers visitors a glimpse into the lives of the Native American tribes who lived in the region many years ago. The museum features exhibits and artifacts that showcase the culture, history, and way of life of the Paiute people.

Other entertainment options include:

- Alchemy Tap Project, Klamath Falls
- Old Mill District, Bend
- Bend Brewfest, Bend
- Fort Rock Village Museum
- High Desert Museum, Bend

Outdoor Recreation

National Forest

Malheur National Forest is in the blue Mountains and covers over 1.7 million acres. The forest is known for its scenic beauty, with rugged mountains, deep canyons, and pristine rivers and streams. The forest is home to a wide range of wildlife including elk, deer, black bears, and mountain lions.

You may also wish to explore:

- Fremont-Winema National Forest
- Deschutes National Forest
- Ochoco National Forest

State Parks and Camping

The popular **Tumalo Canyon State Park** lies along the Deschutes River, just four miles north of Bend. Its central location makes it a good base camp to explore the surrounding attractions. The many crystal-clear streams draw anglers in search of trout. From the parking lot, you can get on the 2.4-mile Deschutes River Trail, which follows the river south through a canyon and past many popular fishing spots.

Smith Rock State Park offers hiking, rock climbing and wildlife watching. This park is a world-renowned destination for rock climbing, with over 1,800 climbing routes. It offers opportunities for climbers of all skill levels, from beginners to experts. The **Misery Ridge Trail** is one of the most popular and challenging trails in the park with breathtaking views of the landscape. For rock formation views, try the **River Trail** hike, an easier path offering scenic views and wildlife. Camping, mountain biking and horseback riding are also available, making Smith Rock Park a perfect destination for a weekend getaway or a longer vacation.

Climbing at Smith Rock, Oregon

Other parks in the area include:

- Pilot Butte State Park
- Prineville State Park
- Lava Lake Campground
- Mazama Village Campground
- Jackson F. Kimball State Recreation Site

For bird lovers, visit the **Malheur National Wildlife Refuge**, a vast wetland complex located in Harney

County. It is home to over 320 species of birds, making it a popular objective for bird watching followers. Visitors can explore the hiking trails, go fishing and enjoy wildlife in its natural habitat.

Other state parks to explore:

- Goose Lake State Recreation Area
- Collier Memorial State Park
- Joseph H Steward State Park and Recreation Area

Treks

The **Steens Mountain Wilderness** is the largest fault block mountain in the northern Great Basin, rising to an elevation of over 9,700 feet. The wilderness spans over 170,000 acres. View the variety of wildlife like big horned sheep, pronghorn, mule deer and golden eagles.
Stats: 9.4 miles, difficult

Other hiking trails include:

- Mount McLoughlin Trail, 9.5 miles, moderate
- Tumalo Mountain Trail, 3.6 miles, moderate

- The Cinder Cone Hiking Area, 4 miles, moderate
- Big Indian Gorge Trail, 10 miles, difficult
- No Name Lake and Ben Glacier, 10.5 miles, difficult

Water Recreation

Lakes
Upper Klamath Lake

This is not only the largest freshwater lake in Oregon but also one of the most beautiful. Some of the largest trout in the country are found here. Pelican Bay, in the northern area of Upper Klamath Lake, is well known among fishermen. There are many canoeing and kayaking trails throughout the marshes.

Crater Lake

Crater Lake, Oregon

This unique lake was formed many years ago when an ancient volcano collapsed, leaving a basin that, over time, filled up with water. The lake's unique geology has created interesting formations like Wizard Island and Phantom Ship, which are best seen aboard a boat while cruising the lake. Hike or bike around the lake and immerse yourself in nature. Fishermen can fish for kokanee salmon or rainbow trout, the only two species found in the lake. The lake is set within Crater Lake National Park.

Other lakes in the area:

- Lake Albert
- Malheur Lake
- Crump Lake
- Summer Lake

Waterfalls

Plunging 272 feet, Watson Falls is one of the highest waterfalls in Oregon. A short trail leads to the lookout for the falls. Be prepared to get wet, as the mist from the waterfall is enough to soak you through.

Susan Creek Falls has a height of approximately 50 feet, making it one of the smaller waterfalls in the Umpqua National Forest. The falls is a series of steps that create a beautiful visual effect.

Other waterfalls to explore include:

- Leslie Gulch – a seasonal waterfall after heavy rain
- Diamond Craters Waterfall
- Alvord Falls
- Kiger Gorge Falls

- Big Indian Gorge Falls
- Wildhorse Lake Falls

Hot Springs

Alvord Hot Springs is a peaceful and relaxing destination that offers visitors a chance to unwind. Visitors can soak in the hot pools and take in the beautiful scenery to enjoy a sense of tranquility that is hard to find elsewhere.

Other hot springs you might enjoy are:

- Crystal Crane Hot springs
- Mickey Hot Springs
- Hart Mountain Hot Springs
- Summer Lake Hot Springs

Alvord Hot Springs, Oregon

Chapter 4: Idaho—The Gem State

Idaho is the gem of the mountains. Its waters are sparkling, and its air is delicious.
If any person wanted to live an outdoor life and enjoy it to the fullest, he could do no better than
to select Idaho as his home."

-Harold G. Wolff

Overview of Idaho

If you think of Idaho, you may think of majestic mountains, rugged forests, and outstretched wilderness, and you wouldn't be wrong; but this state is much more than meets the eye.

Idaho is surrounded by Canada to the north, Montana and Wyoming to the east, Utah and Nevada to the south with Oregon and Washington to the west. The state can be divided into three regions: the Rocky Mountain region in the central northern part, the Columbia Plateau across the southern part, and the Basin and Range Province in the southeast. With more than

4.7 million acres of wilderness, it is not surprising that wildlife is abundant here. From large black bears, mountain sheep, bighorn sheep, and caribou to small ground squirrels, beavers, chipmunks, and pocket mice, they are all prevalent. More than 400 species of birds call this state home, including yellow-billed cuckoos, great horned owls, and Lincoln's sparrows.

Mining played an important part in the history of Idaho. The state's nickname, "Gem State," comes from the more than 72 gems found here. When visiting the old mining town of Silver City, you will be stepping back in time. The city looks exactly like it did in the 1860s, when more than $60 million worth of precious metals were mined here. Logging was another important reason that settlers moved into the area in the 1800s. Many towns and cities lie on the banks of the Snake River for this reason. Today, agriculture still plays an important role. Huge herds of beef cattle and sheep can be found in the prairie regions of the state. The humble potato is the product for which the state is famous. It is said that the first potatoes were introduced to the area by way of Utah during the 1800s. The river valleys and rich volcanic-ash soil provide perfect growing conditions for potatoes. Farmers quickly discovered that potatoes yielded excellent crops of outstanding quality, and Idaho farmers rapidly became leaders in the potato industry. Today, Idaho potato farmers have generations of experience and loads of knowledge about how to grow potatoes successfully. Research into improving soil and storage is ongoing. Idaho boasts some of the world's most advanced storage facilities and remains one of the world's leaders in potato production. Make sure to visit the town of Blackfoot and see the giant baked potato statue in front of the Idaho Potato Museum, a beloved icon of the town.

Idaho has nearly 20,000 miles of trails—more than anyone can walk in their lifetime. Hike through beautiful wilderness land or in the dunes at Bruneau Dunes State Park (climb to the top of the tallest sand dune in North America for an epic view). Descend into Hells Canyon, deeper than the Grand Canyon, and paddle the confluence of the Snake and Salmon Rivers. The term "Great Outdoors" could have been coined for Idaho; there are places to explore everywhere you turn, and around every corner, a new adventure!

You may not have known this, but the Basque population in Idaho is the largest in the United States, dating back to a group of Basques who arrived from Spain in the mid-1800s. These first pioneers were seeking gold but instead found that sheep were big business. And they took to being sheep farmers like fish to water. The Trailing of the Sheep Festival celebrated its 25th anniversary in 2021 and reminds me blatantly of the Fiesta de la Trashumancia in Madrid, Spain (this one is on my bucket list)! The sheep in Spain walk through the streets of Madrid to celebrate the centuries-old tradition of migrating to winter pastures in the fall. In Idaho, the same tradition is celebrated, but it is used as a reason for a very different festival that lasts for a whole weekend and honors not only the sheep migration but also the traditions and cultures of the Basques, Scots, and Peruvians who live in Idaho working on ranches.

Other fun facts about Idaho:

- Idaho had the world's first nuclear powered city, known as "Atomic City," built in southeastern Idaho in the 1950's as part of the government's nuclear energy program.

- Covering over 2.3 million acres, the Frank Church River of No Return Wilderness in Idaho is the largest wilderness area in the contiguous United States.

- The largest potato chip ever made was created in Idaho by the Pringle's company in 1991, measuring 23 inches (53 cm) by 14.5 inches (47 cm).

- Idaho is the only state in the country that is bordered by two navigable rivers: the Snake River and the Clearwater River.

- The famous Hollywood actor, Clint Eastwood was once the mayor of a small town called Sun Valley in Idaho.

- The largest volcanic eruption in the continental United States occurred in Idaho. It created the Craters of the Moon National Monument and Preserve, a landscape of lava field and volcanic cones.

<u>Clever Travel Tips for Your Adventure in Idaho</u>

Idaho
TRAVEL ROUTES, PARKS & PASSES

Travel & Transportation Routes in Idaho

 <u>By Car</u>
- Interstate Highways 95 connects the state from north to south.
- Interstate Highways 90 connect the east and west.

 <u>By Train</u>
The only Amtrak stop in the state arrives and departs daily from Sandpoint:
- Sandpoint Railway Depot

 <u>By Bus</u>
- There are interstate bus services available to Boise and Idaho Falls. The northern part of the state, is spotty: <u>Greyhound.com</u>
- Regional bus services include Coeur d'Alene and Sandpoint: <u>JeffersonLines.com</u>

 <u>By Plane</u>
- There are six airports in Idaho with regular flights throughout the year.
- The major airports are Boise International and Spokane International airports.

Passes & Permits

<u>Idaho State Parks Passport</u> - This pass provides access to all Idaho state parks for one year from the date of purchase. The pass costs $10 for Idaho residents and $40 for non-residents.

The pass can be purchased online at https://idahostateparks.reservea merica.com/home.page

Idaho
WHAT TO PACK &
BEST TIME TO VISIT

Packing Suggestions

<u>Here are some specific items to consider
packing</u>:

- Comfortable Walking Shoes: Idaho offers plenty of opportunities for outdoor activities like hiking, biking, and exploring.
- Water Bottle: Staying hydrated is essential
- Sunscreen and Insect Repellent
- Camera or Smartphone: Idaho's scenic beauty
- Personal Medication
- Warm Clothing: When traveling to Idaho, it's important to pack warm clothes such as jackets, hats, and gloves, even during the summer months. The weather in Idaho can be unpredictable, so it's better to be prepared for cooler temperatures and ensure a comfortable and enjoyable trip.

Best Time to Visit

- The most popular season to visit is summer, the weather is great and the 27 state parks are open with many outdoor activities. Temperature ranges are usually between 75 to 95 degrees.
- Fall from mid-September to November, you will most likely avoid rain and snow. This is a great time for backpacking or hiking adventures!
- Spring is still cool and rain and snow are common in March. From April on, the weather takes a turn and blue skies return.
- Winter brings snow and is a peak time for tourists as there are over 18 ski resorts. Alpine snow activities usually start in late November and end in May.

NORTHERN ID

Northern Idaho Zoom Map

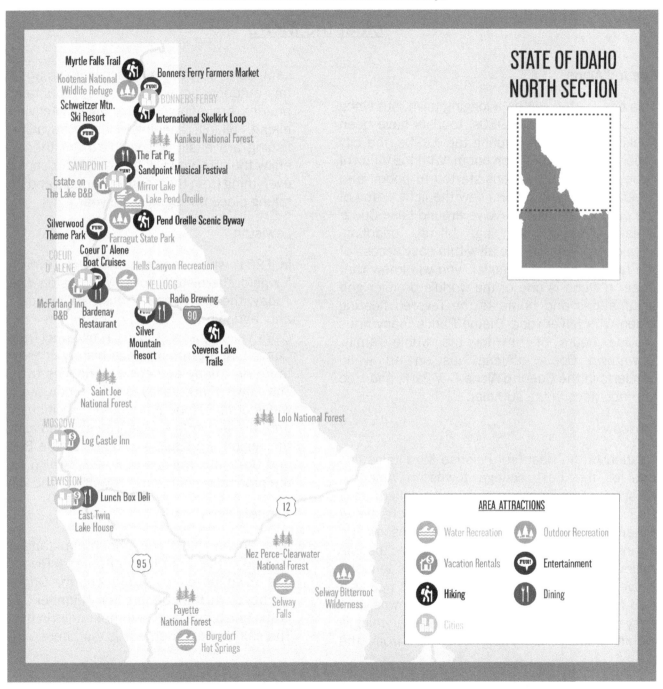

STATE OF IDAHO
NORTH SECTION

Myrtle Falls Trail
Kootenai National Wildlife Refuge
Bonners Ferry Farmers Market
BONNERS FERRY
Schweitzer Mtn. Ski Resort
International Skelkirk Loop
Kaniksu National Forest
The Fat Pig
SANDPOINT
Sandpoint Musical Festival
Estate on The Lake B&B
Mirror Lake
Lake Pend Oreille
Silverwood Theme Park
Pend Oreille Scenic Byway
Farragut State Park
COEUR D'ALENE
Coeur D' Alene Boat Cruises
Hells Canyon Recreation
KELLOGG
McFarland Inn B&B
Bardenay Restaurant
Radio Brewing
90
Silver Mountain Resort
Stevens Lake Trails
Saint Joe National Forest
Lolo National Forest
MOSCOW
Log Castle Inn
LEWISTON
Lunch Box Deli
12
East Twin Lake House
Nez Perce-Clearwater National Forest
95
Payette National Forest
Selway Falls
Selway Bitterroot Wilderness
Burgdorf Hot Springs

AREA ATTRACTIONS

Water Recreation		Outdoor Recreation	
Vacation Rentals		Entertainment	
Hiking		Dining	
Cities			

Section #1 - Northern Idaho

Meet the Metro

Coeur d'Alene

This city started out as a logging town, but since the beginning of the 1980s, tourists have been flocking to the area. During the 1990s, the city experienced a population boom. With the influx of people, tourist attractions started to boom, and several parks and resorts saw the light. Many of the outdoor activities revolve around Lake Coeur d'Alene. Hiking, climbing, biking, paddling, kayaking, or boating are all within easy access of the lake. If you are a golfer, you will know that Coeur d'Alene is one of the world's premier golf destinations and home to the revered floating green. The Silverwood Theme Park's many rides provide hours of fun for the whole family. Downtown Coeur d'Alene has an art walk, concerts in the Coeur d'Alene City Park, and free carriage rides in the summer.

Moscow

Nestled in the beautiful Palouse Mountains lies one of the best college towns in America: Moscow! The city was originally called "Hog Heaven," then "Paradise Valley," before being renamed "Moscow," after the Moscow in Pennsylvania, not Russia, as many people believe. Today, the city is not only home to Idaho University but also a business center as well as a hub for the arts. As with all student towns, it is easy to get around in the city. Nearly everything is within walking or biking distance, from the campus to downtown Moscow. If you are looking for outdoor adventures, the mountains and prairies are a quick drive away. Activities like hiking, biking, running, skiing, kayaking, and fishing are easily accessible from there. If you enjoy the arts, you will be spoiled for choice, with everything from theater to live music and festivals taking place throughout the year.

Lewiston

In 1861, when people came to the area to look for gold, the historic town of Lewiston was built. Today, the city's main industries include timber and agriculture. The city lies within the Lewis Clark Valley, just a stone's throw away from Hells Canyon. Apart from the rich history of the region, there are many outdoor experiences to be had. The Lewis Clark Valley is also renowned for the wines produced here, and the ten wineries in the area are all worth a visit. The soil and climate of the region are similar to those of the Burgundy and Bordeaux regions in France, which explains the production of the high quality of the wines.

Bonners Ferry

Surrounded by three mountain ranges and located in the heart of the Kootenai River Valley, this town oozes old-world charm. Originally a lumber town, the Bonners Ferry Lumber Company is still one of the largest lumber mills in the world. The call of the wilderness is loud here, and once outside, there are countless opportunities to experience the great outdoors. Nearer to town, the historic Pearl Theater is a beautifully remodeled church where artists from all over the area come to perform. The scenic downtown area has many boutiques and eateries to visit.

Sand Point

Mountains, green valleys, and the largest lake in Idaho can all be found near Sand Point. There are many hiking and biking trails, as well as several private campgrounds with RV parks nearby. In winter, many cross-country skiers flock to the area to try their skills on the countless groomed trails. For family fun, be sure to visit the Silverwood Theme Park with more than 70 rides. The most famous is called the Aftershock, a 191-foot-tall roller coaster that reaches speeds of up to 65 mph as it speeds through the cobra rolls and inverted loops. For water-sport enthusiasts, both lakes and rivers offer many adventures: whitewater rafting, boating, kayaking, and fishing, as well as motorized sports like jet skis and fishing charters.

Entrées and Edibles

Bardenay Restaurant and Distillery, Coeur d'Alene

This restaurant has an on-site distillery that produces spirits made with care. The Coeur d'Alene distillery produces vodka, gin, and liqueurs. Spirits are made in small batches and are regularly tasted throughout the distilling process. The lunch and dinner menu in the restaurant has flavors from around the globe; try the Mediterranean plate, the Portuguese clams, or the Teriyaki Salmon Satay.

The Fat Pig, Sand Point

An eclectic and seasonally rotating menu using locally sourced ingredients. They also have a large craft beer and wine list making this a unique eatery. The menu includes dishes like Korean barbecue chicken tenders and pork ramen. Eat inside or sit on the patio next to the firepit for an evening of delicious food and drinks.

Lunch Box Deli, Lewiston

Located in a bright red building, you cannot miss the Lunch Box Deli. The atmosphere is laid-back, and the staff is friendly and helpful. If you visit more than once, don't be surprised to be greeted by name. The sandwiches and BBQ dishes come highly recommended!

Radio Brewing, Kellogg

Friendly service and an old-time radio ambiance are some of the reasons this restaurant is so popular. Their craft beers are named after radio shows that aired between the 1920s and the 1950s. The brewery was the first to open in the town of Kellogg and has quickly become a favorite with visitors and locals alike.

Vacation Homes

The McFarland Inn Bed and Breakfast, Coeur d'Alene

Located on a quiet street in the historic Garden District of Coeur d'Alene, this beautiful home offers five luxury guest rooms. Situated within walking distance of Lake Coeur d'Alene and the vibrant downtown, commuting is easy. A full breakfast is served in the dining room, which overlooks an opulent garden.

Estate on the Lake, Bed and Breakfast, Dover

This true lakefront home offers visitors an extraordinary experience, located on the lakeside with spectacular views of the Gold Mountain and the Cabinet Mountains. Enjoy the pergola flower gardens and waterfall fishpond. Sit on the dock and enjoy the wildlife sauntering past. The property offers three luxurious suites, each with waterfront views, hi-tech entertainment centers, and marble- clad bathrooms.

Log Castle Inn, Moscow Mountain

Experience the handcrafted log home in the woods. Visitors will feel that they are relaxing in the wilderness. Wildlife regularly visits the area, and visitors may see deer, moose, and turkeys. Guests may access the pine forest at the back of the cottage, where many hiking and biking trails can be found.

Sandpoint Cottage, Sandpoint

The brand-new two-bedroom apartment is in town, close to everything you could want. Stroll downtown to visit the breweries and coffee shops or take a drive to Schweitzer Mountain Ski Resort. The apartment is fully equipped and pet-friendly. Bring your bikes, skis, or kayaks and enjoy the nature around you.

East Twin Lake House, Lewiston

This property is ideally suited for families as is situated on the lake. Lewiston and the East Twin Public Beach are just minutes away. Visitors can enjoy the fire pit, large deck, and use the canoe and kayak.

Entertainment and Tourism

Silverwood Theme Park, Athol

If you are looking for family fun, look no further. The Silverwood Theme Park has rides and slides for everyone. From the vintage vehicles idly cruising along on their track to the "stunt pilot" plunging 105 feet to the ground, there are rides for every taste. For fun in the water, Boulder Beach Bay has two enormous wave pools, while Elkhorn Creek offers a lazy tube ride downriver. For another form of entertainment, watch one of the award-winning shows. With Mad Mike as your host, the High Moon Saloon is a magical place.

Silver Mountain Resort, Kellogg

This resort is open all year and offers activities for every season. The resort has skiing, snowboarding, snow tubing, and snowshoeing onsite and guests can hike, bike, or even book a gondola ride. The resort also has ziplines, rafting, and four-wheelers for rent. The Kids Passport gives little one's access to a host of activities like outdoor movies, water bomb fights, camp-fire singalongs, and much more.

Coeur d'Alene Boat Cruises

Take a scenic boat ride on Lake Coeur d'Alene and experience the beautiful surroundings from the water. An experienced captain will act as a tour guide on the trip. You will be able to peek at the secluded mansions as you venture into the Spokane and St. Joe Rivers for a relaxing half-day cruise.

Other entertainment options in the area include:

- Ziplining, Coeur d'Alene
- Bonner's Ferry Farmers Market
- Igloos on the lake, Coeur d'Alene
- Sandpoint Musical Festival
- Coeur d'Alene Resort Golf Resort
- Wallace District Mining Museum
- Idaho Shakespeare Festival

Outdoor Recreation

Kaniksu National Forest

This forest is in the panhandle of Idaho and covers 1.6 million acres. It has beautiful

mountains, rocky outcrops, wildflower meadows, and two charming towns. Popular activities include hiking, biking, off-road vehicles, water sports, and camping. The forest is home to an abundance of wildlife, such as moose, black bears, and the endangered caribou. There are eight different campsites in the forest, most of which are near a lake or stream. If you prefer the luxury of a cabin, you have a choice between cabins in the mountains or lower-lying cabins near streams.

Camping

Farragut State Park

The 4,000-acre park offers 223 camping sites, a number of group camping sites, as well as several camping cabins. Hiking in the park is family-friendly, with clear and interpretive signs throughout. In the summer, hiking, biking, water sports, and archery are popular, while snowy winters offer plenty of cross-country skiing possibilities.

Other camping possibilities include:

- Mirror Lake Campground
- Camp Victoria

Treks

International Selkirk Loop

Why not take a 280-mile scenic road trip through the Selkirk Mountains? The loop takes travelers into Canada while following the rivers and lakes that were historically used for transportation. The beauty of the region is spectacular, and you will experience the longest ferry ride on the continent when crossing Kootenay Lake. Along the way, there are a lot of places to stay, from campgrounds to motels to high-end hotels. If you are looking for a unique road trip, this is it!

Pend Oreille Scenic Byway is a beautiful driving route that stretches for 33 miles along the pend Oreille River in northern Idaho. There are several hiking trails and outdoor recreational opportunities in the area.

Some of the more popular hiking trails include:

- Trail #65, 5.5 miles, moderate
- Myrtle Falls Trail, 0.3 miles, easy
- Ross Creek Cedars Trail, 0.9 miles, easy
- Gold Hill North Trail, 6.5 miles, moderate

Idaho Panhandle National Forest

World-class fisheries are supported by vast lakes and miles of rivers. The forest is abundant with wildlife and is home to big game. You will find elk, deer, caribou, even grizzly bears, and wolves. The Idaho Panhandle has a rich history that continues to connect families to mountains and vast bodies of water.

Heyburn State Park

Lakes, meadows, forests, and marshlands are all found in the 8,000-acre park. Hiking and biking trails are available all year. The popular Trail of the Coeur d'Alene's runs through the park and attracts mountain bikers from all over the country. The park has three scenic lakes that offer many opportunities for swimming, boating, canoeing, kayaking, and fishing.

Other campgrounds include:

- Riley Creek Campground
- Green Bay Campground
- Priest Lake State Park
- Mirror Lake Campground

Treks

Steven Lakes Trail is a short but quite steep trail that leads to two crystal-clear lakes at the foot of Stevens Peak in the Bitterroot Mountains. The area is best known for the annual Spokane Mountaineers' Mountain School held each spring. Mountaineers can practice crampon use and rope travel as they ascend Stevens Peak. *Stats: 4.8 miles, moderate*

Other (more traditional) treks in the area include:

- Mineral Ridge National Recreation Trail, 3.3 mile, moderate
- Pulaski Tunnel Trail, 4.5 miles, moderate
- Ross Creek Cedars Trail, 1.5 miles, easy
- Scotchman Peak Trail, 7.5 miles, difficult

Coeur d'Alene National Forest

This forest is a 726,000-acre forest offering a wide range of outdoor recreational opportunities, including hiking, fishing, hunting, camping and winter sports. Home to several lakes and rivers, it features rugged mountain terrain, dense forests, and abundant wildlife.

It includes the well-known Lake Coeur d'Alene, a large scenic lake offering boating, fishing, swimming, and hiking. The lake is also home to several resorts, golf courses and hosts an annual holiday light display which features over a million lights and attracts visitors from all over the world.

Camping

Wolf Lodge Campground is situated in a beautiful, forested area. It offers access to Coeur d'Alene Lake with nearby hiking trails and outdoor recreational activities. The campground has a variety of camping options, including tent and RV sites. There are several amenities such as picnic tables, fire pits, restrooms, and showers. It also has a boat launch and dock making it easy to enjoy the lake.

Other campgrounds to consider are:

- Beauty Creek Campground
- Kootenai County Fairground RV Park
- Big Hank Campground
- Blackwell Island RV Park

Treks

- Coeur d'Alene Trail, 32 miles, easy
- Tubbs Hill Trail, 2.2 miles, moderate
- Mineral Ridge National Recreation Trail, 3.3 miles, moderate
- Hiawatha Trail, 15 miles, easy

Lolo National Forest

Lolo National Forest covers over 2 million acres of wilderness, mountains, and lakes. The forest offers endless opportunities for outdoor recreation including hiking, fishing, hunting, camping, and skiing. Selway-Bitterroot Wilderness and Rattlesnake Wilderness are popular remote areas providing a rugged setting for backpacking, camping, and back country activities.

Camping

Trout Creek Campground is situated on the shore of Lake Pend Oreille, which is the largest lake in Idaho. The campground offers stunning views of the lake and is surrounded by mountains. It has easy access to water-based activities such as boating, fishing, and swimming. Several hiking trails are nearby for exploration and adventure. Amenities offered include a picnic table, fire rings, vault toilets, drinking water, day use area, a boat ramp, and a fish cleaning station.

Other campgrounds for your enjoyment are:

- Dalles Campground
- Harry's Flat Campground
- Fish Creek Campground
- Wendover Campground
- Jerry Johnson Campground

Treks

- Morrell Falls National Recreation Area, 7 miles, moderate
- Heart and Pearl Lakes Trail, 7.8 miles, moderate
- Blossom Lakes Trail, 6.2 miles, moderate
- Scotchman Peak Trail, 7 miles, difficult
- Trout Creek Trail, 7 miles, moderate

St. Joe National Forest

The Saint Joe National Forest is known for its rugged mountains, pristine lakes, and extensive trail network. Visitors can explore the area on foot, horseback or mountain bike and can enjoy fishing, hunting, and camping in the forest.

Camping

Lost Moose Campground has a rustic atmosphere. It features primitive campsites with fire rings and picnic tables. There is no running water at the campground so visitors must bring their own water or treat water from the nearby river. The campground has vault toilets which are simple and basic. It is located near the banks of the St. Joe River and offers beautiful views of the surrounding forested mountains.

Other campgrounds include:

- Marble Creek Campground
- Bald Mountain Lookout Campground
- Shadowy St. Joe Campground
- Shoshone Campground

Treks

The **Lone Lake Trail** is a well-known hike in the Selkirk Mountains. The trek winds through beautiful forests and meadows, offering views of the many mountain peaks. The highlight of the trail is the clear Lone Lake, a refreshing spot for swimming or fishing.
Stats: 6 miles, moderate

Other treks include:

- Elk River Backcountry, 28 miles, moderate
- Stevens Lake Loop Trail, 5.5 miles, moderate
- Mallard Larkins Snow Peak Loop, 22 miles, difficult

Nez Perce Clearwater National Forest

The Nez Perce Clearwater National Forest offers stunning natural beauty with unspoiled mountains, lakes, wild rivers, deep canyons, and rugged peaks. It covers over 4 million acres with over nine designated wilderness areas. A rich diversity of wildlife including elk, moose, grizzly bears, and gray wolves call this forest home. It is also rich in cultural history, with many archaeological sites and historic landmarks related to the Nez Perce people.

Camping

Rocky Ridge Lake Campground offers numerous amenities for visitors, including picnic areas, fire pits, and a boat ramp for easy access to the lake. The surrounding area offers excellent opportunities for hiking, fishing, and wildlife watching. Visitors can also explore nearby historic landmarks, including the ghost town of Rocky Bar and the mining town of Atlanta. The campground offers potable water, picnic tables, and fire rings making it an ideal spot for camping in the fresh outdoors.

Other campgrounds recommended:

- Wilderness Getaway
- Washington Creek Campground

- Lochsa River Campground
- Powell Campground
- Kelly Forks Campground

Canyon Deer in Idaho

Treks

- Sheep Lake Shortcut, 3.5 miles, moderate
- Rocky Ridge Trail, 3.5 miles, moderate
- Elk Mountain Trail, 7 miles, difficult
- Lolo Creek Trail, 9 miles, moderate
- Fish Creek Trail, 7.5 miles, moderate

Selway-Bitterroot Wilderness

The Selway Bitterroot Wilderness is spread between Idaho and Montana spanning over 1.3 million acres of stunning mountainous landscapes, pristine lakes like Painted Rocks Lake and Heart Lake, and flowing rivers like Selway, Lochsa, and Middle Fork of the Salmon. It contains ten peaks over 10,000 feet tall, including Trapper Peak, the highest peak in the Bitterroot Range. The area is home to abundant wildlife like grizzly bear, black bear, wolves, elk, and mountain lions. It is a popular destination for hiking (over 1,600 miles of trails), camping, and fishing. Visitors can explore the vast wilderness and enjoy its rugged, natural beauty.

Camping

- Warm Springs Creek Campground
- Moose Creek Campground
- Big Creek Lake Campground

Camping – Dispersed

Painted Rock Reservoir offers camping on the shores of the reservoir. You won't want to miss the stunning views of wildflowers at Painted Rock in the spring and the abundance of trout fishing in the reservoir.

Moose Creek offers camping near the riverbank and is known for its world-class fly-fishing opportunities particularly with cutthroat and rainbow trout.

Warm Springs Creek offers stunning views of the mountains and wildlife galore. The area around Warm Springs is known for its hot springs, which are located just upstream from the camping area offering a relaxing destination for soaking in a natural setting.

White Cap Creek is popular with backcountry enthusiasts, with several trails leading into the wilderness from nearby trailheads. It is known for its rugged and remote terrain.

Treks

- Magruder Corridor Trail, 100 miles long, various levels
- West Fork Fish Creek Trail, 16 miles, moderate
- Moose Creek Trail, 36 miles, difficult
- Jerry Johnson Hot Springs Trail, 5 miles, easy
- Painted Rock Lake Trail, 14 miles, moderate

Payette National Forest, Idaho

Payette National Forest

This national forest is a diverse and unique landscape covering over 2.3 million acres of wilderness. It is known for its rough terrain which includes the Salmon River Range and the high plateau of the Camas Prairie. The forest is home to many animals including elk, deer, black bear, mountain goats and wolves. It also boasts over

300 lakes and reservoirs, offering a variety of recreational opportunities such as boating, fishing, and swimming. There are many trails for visitors to explore that offer breathtaking views. The forest is rich in cultural history, with evidence of Native American habitation dating back many years.

Camping

Ponderosa State Park located on the western shore of Payette Lake has 55 campsites. This lake is one of the deepest natural lakes in Idaho with a depth of 392 feet. The campground is named after the Pine trees that surround the area. These trees can grow up to 200 feet tall and are known for their orange bark. The campground is known for its variety of bird species such as ospreys, bald eagles and great blue herons. The amenities include picnic tables, fire rings, drinking water, flush toilets, and a boat ramp.

North Fork Campground, located in the Payette River Scenic Byway offers remarkable panoramas of the river and the mountains. The campground is situated near the river which is famous for its world-class whitewater rafting opportunities. It is a great starting point for hiking to the remote beauty of Boulder Lake, which offers breathtaking views of the surrounding forest and the nearby Salmon River Mountains. The amenities include 17 campsites, picnic tables, fire rings, vault toilets and drinking water. While it is a smaller campground, it provides a peaceful and secluded camping experience.

Additional campsites to explore:

- Sagehen Reservation Campground
- Brundage Reservoir Campground
- French Creek Campground
- Lake Cascade State Park

Treks

- Boulder Loop Trail, 3.5 miles, moderate
- Goat Mountain Trail, 6 miles, difficult
- Rapid River Trail, 14 miles, difficult
- Louie Lake Trail, 6.4 miles, moderate
- Box Lake Trail, 4.5 miles, moderate

Recreation Sites
Kootenai National Wildlife Refuge

This 2,774-acre refuge offers a variety of habitats for a wide diversity of animals and is nestled next to the Selkirk Mountains in northern Idaho. The refuge is relatively small, but it contains a diversity of habitat types that are vital to the high number of wildlife species that use it throughout the migrating and breeding seasons.

Hells Canyon Recreation Area

This national treasure, which straddles the borders of northeastern Oregon and western Idaho, contains acres of beauty and adventure where you can let your senses go as wild as the surroundings! This is one of North America's deepest river gorges and includes landscapes that are as stunning as any on the continent. The area is renowned for whitewater rafting, and enthusiasts travel from far for the experience. Magnificent mountain peaks and vast wilderness areas that can be explored on foot or on horseback. Whether you decide to experience Hells Canyon National Recreation Area on foot, horseback, or raft, we are confident that you will find it to be a truly remarkable area.

Schweitzer Mountain Ski Resort, a year-round destination for outdoor enthusiasts. In the winter, visitors can ski or snowboard on the resorts' 2,900 acres of skiable terrain. The resort's summit is over 6,000 feet above sea level and offers panoramic views of the surrounding mountains. The terrain includes groomed runs, glades, and terrain parks. In the summer, visitors can hike, bike, and play disc golf. The resort features several restaurants and spas.

The 15-mile rail-to-trail mountain bike route that runs through the **Bitterroot Mountains** is the Hiawatha Trail. It features tunnels, trestles, and stunning views of the surrounding landscape. The trail runs through dense forests crossing several streams, sand, and waterfalls. The trail has a gentle grade and smooth surface that is suitable for all ages and abilities.

Other things to do in the area:

- Rock Climbing near Post Falls
- Fishing in Northern Idaho
- Brundage Mountain Ski Resort
- Sun Valley Ski Resort

Water Recreation

Lakes

Lake Pend Oreille, the largest and deepest in Idaho. It is located between three ranges of the Rocky Mountains and has beautiful natural scenery. There are many recreational opportunities, with plenty of picnic sites, boat launches, and fishing. The lake is known for Kamloops (a giant rainbow trout) and salmon.

Other lakes in the area include:

- Priest Lake
- Spirit Lake Feet
- Harrison Lake

Lake Pend Orielle, Idaho

Waterfalls

Elk Creek Falls has three beautiful waterfalls; the lowest has a 20-foot drop and the highest has a full 70-foot drop. The falls are easily accessible by three well maintained trails.

A friend of mine, Evan, has a favorite story to tell about the time he (a real city slicker) booked a horseback trail ride to explore the falls. He had never ridden before and was extremely nervous, but the ranger assured him that he was on the oldest and calmest horse in the yard and would be fine. Everything went well for most of the ride, but just before the falls, they encountered a family with their dogs off-leash, and the horses became jittery. Evan managed to keep his horse under control, but when a huge Great Dane came bounding up from behind, his horse took off. According to Evan, the ground flew past, and all he could see was the waterfall closing in. The horse was able to stop at the water's edge, but poor Evan was thrown wide and ended up in the pool below a waterfall. He was drenched but happy to be alive, and he decided there and then to never get on a horse again.

Other waterfalls to explore nearby:

- Shadow Falls
- Bull Run Creek Falls
- Shoestring Falls
- Selway Falls

Elk Creek Falls, Idaho

Trail Creek Hot Springs, Idaho

Hot Springs
Burgdorf Hot Springs

If you are looking for a rustic getaway, you may enjoy what Burgdorf has to offer. The springs are in the Payette National Forest, where you can see the beautiful mountains all around. There are three historic hot spring pools with log sides and gravel bottoms.

Additional hot springs to explore:

- Stanley Hot Springs
- Jerry John Weir Creek Hot Springs
- Goldbug Hot Springs
- Lolo Hot Springs
- Council Mountain Hot Springs
- Trail Creek Hot Springs

SOUTHERN ID

Southern Idaho Zoom Map

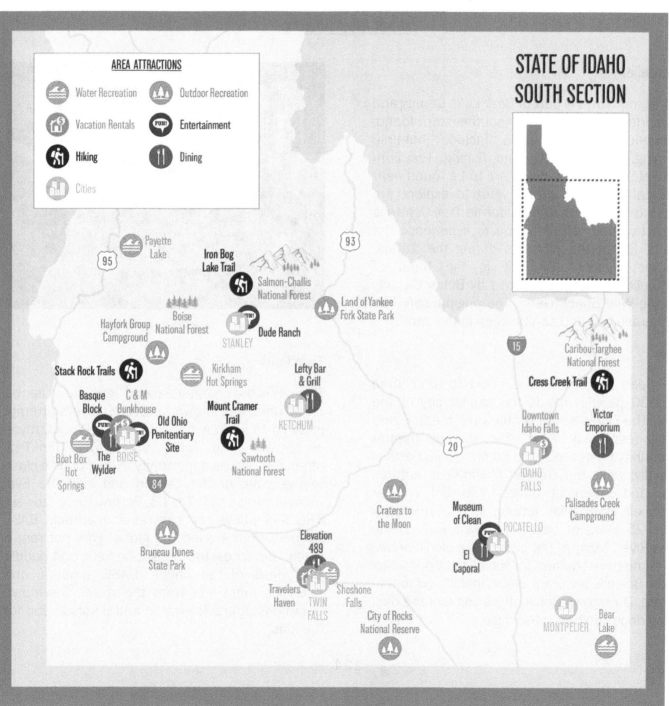

AREA ATTRACTIONS

- Water Recreation
- Vacation Rentals
- Hiking
- Cities
- Outdoor Recreation
- Entertainment
- Dining

STATE OF IDAHO
SOUTH SECTION

Payette Lake

95

93

Iron Bog Lake Trail

Salmon-Challis National Forest

Land of Yankee Fork State Park

Hayfork Group Campground

Boise National Forest

STANLEY

Dude Ranch

15

Caribou-Targhee National Forest

Stack Rock Trails

Kirkham Hot Springs

Lefty Bar & Grill

Cress Creek Trail

Basque Block

C & M Bunkhouse

Mount Cramer Trail

KETCHUM

Downtown Idaho Falls

Victor Emporium

Old Ohio Penitentiary Site

Boat Box Hot Springs

The Wylder

BOISE

Sawtooth National Forest

20

IDAHO FALLS

Palisades Creek Campground

84

Craters to the Moon

Museum of Clean

POCATELLO

Bruneau Dunes State Park

Elevation 489

El Caporal

Travelers Haven

TWIN FALLS

Shoshone Falls

City of Rocks National Reserve

MONTPELIER

Bear Lake

Section #2 - Southern Idaho

Meet the Metro

Montpelier

This historic town is part of Bear Lake County and is the ideal base to explore southeastern Idaho. Experiences in the area include hunting, camping, hiking, skiing, and fishing. Premium bird-watching opportunities are to be found near Bear Lake Marina. If you want to explore the history of the region, the California Trail Centre is interactive and will allow you to experience the way of life of the pioneers during the 1800s. Another museum to visit is the Bank of Montpelier, which was robbed by Butch Cassidy and the Wild Bunch Gang. The original safe has been preserved and can be seen in the bank.

Boise City Lights, Idaho

Boise

The green city of Boise is home to more than 235,000 people and is the capital city of the state. The city is a hub for the arts, theater, and music (especially jazz). The vibrant theater community hosts the Idaho Shakespeare Festival annually, while the Treefort Music Fest features local and emerging bands. The Boise River Greenbelt is popular among locals. This park offers 25 miles of paved pathways next to the Boise River. Many of the parks have picnic areas, and some have shelters for social gatherings. City center Boise is a vibrant place, inviting visitors to explore. Downtown Boise offers some of the best dining opportunities in the region.

Twin Falls

This city is the commercial and agricultural center of the area. It is known for Evel Knievel's attempt in 1974 to jump across the Snake River Canyon on his sky cycle. Today, the Canyon Rim Trail offers visitors the opportunity to hike or bike close to the edge of the canyon and visit the Evel Knievel launch site. The I.B. Perrine Bridge towers 486 feet above the canyon and attracts BASE jumpers from around the globe. Why not rent a kayak and follow the Shoshone Falls and paddle with views of the bridge, BASE jumpers, and Knievel's jump site from the river? Downtown Commons offers live music and a splash pad for the kids.

Pocatello

For many, this city is a stopover to Yellowstone National Park. But the city is worth a longer visit; it is nestled in the mountains with many outdoor activities. It is ideally located as the base for a number of well-known outdoor destinations and was on National Geographic's list of the "100 Best Adventure Towns" in 2009 (National Geographic, 2011). Most hotels are centrally located. One attraction is the Idaho Falls Riverwalk, a paved walk next to the Snake River.

Entrées and Edibles

The Wilder, Boise

The restaurant was opened in 2017 and boasts a 52-year-old sourdough starter still used for pizza dough, muffins, and breads baked on-site. Cozy seating is available at the bistro tables or at the bar.

El Caporal Mexican Restaurant, Pocatello

This family-owned restaurant brings authentic Mexican flavors to downtown Pocatello. The restaurant is family friendly and caters to spice lovers as well as those who don't like it too hot. But be warned: spicy means hot!!

We stopped by a couple of years ago with friends on our way to Yellowstone Park. Our European friends were keen to try out "authentic Mexican cuisine," and although we tried to warn them about the heat that goes with "spicy," they ordered a Three Chile Carne. They tried hard to keep their composure, but soon their faces were red with tears streaming down their cheeks. They did not finish the main course and opted for ice cream as they did not trust the Mexican churros or sopapillas, even though we tried to reassure them they were not spicy! Now it is an inside joke in our family: If something is very spicy, we call it "Three Chile Carne."

Elevation 489, Twin Falls

This elegant bistro offers delicious cuisine from around the world. The patio seating and firepit have breathtaking views of the mountains. The dinner menu includes regional delicacies like Dungeness crab and Idaho trout.

Lefty Bar and Grill, Ketchum

The quant building has been serving delicious burgers and subs for twenty years. The warm atmosphere and sunny outside deck make it a favorite for a meal or catching up with friends.

Victor Emporium, Idaho Falls

This small-town store not only has the best ice cream and milkshakes, but you can also find fishing supplies, souvenirs, and even sunglasses! The Victor Emporium is famous for its huckleberry milkshake and old-time soda fountain.

Vacation Houses

C&M Bunkhouse, Boise

This guesthouse is close to the Arrowrock Dam and the Bogus Basin Ski Resort. The rooms are luxuriously decorated and boast air conditioning as well as fireplaces. Coffee and tea makers, as well as a turndown service, are just a few of the ways the management ensures your stay is unforgettable.

Traveler Haven, Twin Falls

The house is truly the perfect getaway. The canyon and downtown are just a few minutes away by car. The house has two bedrooms and a large living area and outdoor patio.

Twin Falls Modern Retreat, Twin Falls

Just 2.9 kilometers away from the College of Southern Idaho, this home is centrally located. The house has a game room that comes with an old-school arcade game and a patio with a firepit. Whether you are just passing through or planning a longer stay, you will be comfortable here.

Downtown Idaho Falls

This tastefully decorated holiday home comfortably sleeps five people in its three bedrooms. The modern kitchen is well equipped, and the laundry room has a washer and dryer, ideal for those cold, wet winter days. The house is pet-friendly and has plenty of outdoor space for your four-legged friends.

Entertainment and Tourism

Basque Block Population

Although The Basque Block is located on just one block in downtown Boise, its effects are felt all over the world! The Basque Block is the home of the Basque culture in Boise, and the 16,000 people living there are the largest community in the country. It served as a sort of new home for many of the Basques who immigrated to Idaho in the 1800s and stayed there until the end of the Franco era in Spain.

Dude Ranch Experience, Stanley

Experience the Idaho prairies from horseback on a guided trail ride. Cast a line in one of the trout streams or lakes. You can even join an "Intro to Fly Fishing" class and learn how to cast and tie the basic knots you will need when fly fishing. Other activities offered include lawn games, target shooting, archery, and arts and crafts.

Kathy and her family had been dreaming of a true Western experience and they finally found it at the dude ranch in Idaho. They spent their days riding horses and hiking the trails, but it was fly fishing that captivated Kathy. She was fascinated by the skill of tying knots and the precision required to cast the line. With the help of one of the ranch's ever so attractive guides, she was soon

reeling in fish after fish. The feeling of accomplishment was exhilarating. But the fun did not stop there. Kathy and her family also tried their hand at target shooting and archery, competing against one another in friendly tournaments. The competition was fierce, as her dad was always so competitive and did not want to lose. As they gathered around the campfires each night, sharing stories and roasting marshmallows, Kathy knew that this experience had brought her family even closer together and created memories that would last a lifetime.

Old Penitentiary Site

The historic prison building dates back to 1870 and was used to house inmates until 1973. Today, visitors can experience a little bit of what it was like to be incarcerated there. The museum houses artifacts from escape attempts and general prison life during the 103 years the prison was in use.

Snake River Wine Region is home to over 50 wineries and vineyards. Visitors can take wine tours, sample local wines, from classic reds and whites to unique blends and experimental varieties. Enjoy the beautiful view of the surrounding countryside and the Snake River.

Discovery Center

The center aims to provide hands-on science education to youth. The center hosts many traveling exhibitions from around the world in addition to creating their own. It also provides spring and summer learning camps.

Other entertainment options include:

- Idaho Black History Museum
- Aquarium of Boise
- Museum of Clean
- Idaho Botanical Gardens
- Freak Alley Gallery

Outdoor Recreation

Being in nature reminds me of words from the Bible:
(New International Version)

Psalm 8:3: "When I see and consider Your heavens, the work of Your fingers, the moon and the stars, which You have established!"

Psalm 96:11 and 12:12: "Let the heavens be glad, and let the earth rejoice; let the sea roar, and all that is in it, let the field exult, and everything in it! Then shall all the trees of the forest sing for joy."

City of Rocks

A very unique "city," where the towering skyscrapers are granite towers, and the

127

residents have four legs or wings. Climbers come from all over the globe to climb the granite of Almo Pluton. This city offers 700 opportunities for climbers, but also many hiking and biking trails. In winter, snowshoeing and skiing are popular ways to explore the area's unique geological features.

🔭 *Many years ago, I was convinced by a (then) boyfriend who was a climber to accompany him to the City of Rocks. I was planning a weekend of reading and gentle hiking while the man in my life ascended the heights. On the very first morning, he begged me to accompany him and just climb a small outcrop. Now, my fear of spiders is only surpassed by my fear of heights. The boyfriend assured me I would be fine as long as I didn't look down. Easier said than done; I was a few very steep steps from the top when I thought I heard something below, and I looked down—and instantly froze. It took a very irritated boyfriend nearly half the morning to get me back on solid ground. Needless to say, he decided to leave the climbing for himself which gave me the perfect opportunity to delve into my book!*

Salmon Challis National Forest

This unique and diverse forest covers over 4.3 million acres of land, making it one of the largest national forests in the country. It is named after two major rivers that flow through it: the Salmon River and the Challis River. The Salmon River runs through the heart of the forest and is one of the longest undammed rivers in the contiguous United States. The forest landscape is unique in that it includes high mountain peaks and low-lying valleys. Camping, hiking, and fishing are plentiful.

Camping

Screech Owl, Idaho

Land of the Yankee State Park is in the heart of Idaho's mining country. Exhibits, interpretive trails, and guided tours of the historic buildings offer a unique experience to this camping spot. Do not forget the many outdoor recreational opportunities it offers like biking, fishing, and hiking trails.

Additional camping locations include:

- Challis Bridge Campground
- North Fork Campground
- Morgan Creek Campground

Treks

- Kane Lake Trail, 3.5 miles, moderate
- Iron Bog Lake Trail, 4.4 miles, easy
- Blue Lake Trail, 6 miles, moderate

Boise National Forest

This large park spans over 2.5 million acres of wilderness. Explore the forests, grasslands, the North Fork Payette River Canyon, and Trinity Mountain. There are more than 500 trails to choose from, and water enthusiasts have a choice of 250 lakes and reservoirs. Boise National Forest is home to several hot springs that offer a relaxing and rejuvenating experience.

Camping

Hayfork Group Campground lies at the foot of a hillside covered in pine. Mores Creek runs nearby and is a great place to fish for trout. Other things to do there include hiking, biking, and horseback riding. In the snowy season, backcountry skiers visit to hone their skills.

Three Sisters Group Campground is in the Boise National Forest in western Idaho. It sits at an elevation of approximately 6,500 feet above sea level. The campground is named after the Three Sisters Peaks, which are nearby and rise to an elevation of over 9,000 feet. The peaks are a popular destination for hikers of all levels. The area is popular for fishing, hiking, mountain biking and wildlife viewing, and the nearby lake Cascade offers boating and other water activities.

Other campgrounds nearby include:

- Pine Flats Campground
- Park Creek Campground
- Sage Hen Reservoir Campground
- Ponderosa Campground

Treks

Stack Rock Trail is named after a unique rock formation that hikers will come across on the trail. The formation looks like a stack of rocks or pillars, which makes it a popular spot for photos and a unique landmark to look for along the trail. Hikers may encounter mule deer, elk, black bears, and a variety of bird species, including blue jays and woodpeckers. This makes the trail not only a scenic and challenging hike, but also an opportunity to observe and appreciate the natural beauty of the area.

Stats: 5.5 miles, moderate

Olympic Marmot, Photo by Romy Hoffman

129

Other treks include:

- Shafer Butte Trail, 7.6 miles, moderate
- Stack Rock Trail, 5.5 miles, moderate
- Beaver Creek Trail, 6.8 miles, moderate
- Redfish Lake Trail, 4.2 miles, easy
- Grandjean Trail, 10.6 miles, difficult

Sawtooth National Forest

The Sawtooth National Recreation Area is a picturesque mountainous area. It has more than 700 miles of trails, 40 peaks that rise beyond 10,000 feet, and more than 300 high mountain lakes all contribute to the area's breathtaking backdrop and scenery. Some recreational activities are camping, hiking, backpacking, fishing, rafting, watching nature, and bike riding.

Camping

Easley Campground is in the shade of lush Cottonwood and Aspen trees. The Big Wood River flows next to the campground, and in summer, the riverbanks are covered in wildflowers. The Easley Resort is a campground with a warm swimming pool. There are many outdoor activities like hiking, biking, and fishing.

Other campgrounds include:

- Sawtooth National Recreation Area
- Chemeketan Campground
- Redfish Lake Campground
- Stanley Lake Campground

Sawtooth Mountain Range, Idaho

Treks

Mount Cramer Trail's summit lies on the border between Custer and Boise counties. The Hell Roaring Lake Trailhead allows climbers to summit the mountain in one day. The standard route is via the southwest ridge, which is a strenuous and technical climb that requires rock climbing skills. *Stats: 16 miles, difficult*

Other hikes include:

- Snake River Trail, 10 miles, moderate
- Stanley Lake Bridal Veil Falls Trail, 3.5 miles, easy to moderate
- Sawtooth Scenic Byway scenic drive, 115 miles
- Castle Peak Trails, 12 miles, difficult
- Fishhook Creek Trail, 13 miles, moderate
- Alpine Way Trail, 9 miles, moderate
- Pettit Lake Trail, 6.4 miles, easy
- Redfish Lake Trail, 4.2 miles, easy

Caribou Targhee National Forest

Caribou-Targhee National Forest is included in parts of Idaho and Wyoming. It is a vast and diverse region covering over 3 million acres. One of its most unique characteristics is its geology, which includes the Teton fault, the Yellowstone hotspot, and the Caribou Mountains volcanic field. Visitors can explore numerous caves, canyons, hot springs, and lava fields. The forest is also home to a diverse range of wildlife, including moose, elk, grizzly bears, and wolves. The forest is also famous for its beautiful wildflowers and scenic drives, including the Teton Scenic Byway and the Mesa Falls Scenic Byway.

Camping

Palisades Campground located near the Palisades Reservoir has 68 sites and offers access to fishing, boating, and hiking. The sites are spacious, offering amenities such as fire rings, picnic tables and drinking water.

The Teton Canyon Campground has 17 sites and has access to hiking, fishing, and mountain biking. The sites are first-come, first-served and offer amenities such as fire rings, picnic tables and vault toilets.

Other options include:

- Henry's Lake State Park
- Fairway RV Park
- Snake River RV Park and Campground

Snake River Rapids, Idaho

Treks

Cress Creek Trail takes you through a remarkable forest with views of the Teton Range. The trailhead is located near Teton Canyon and the hike features a steady incline until you reach the beautiful Cross Creek waterfall.
Stats: 4.8 miles, moderate
Experience one of the most incredible drives in the United States, the **Teton Scenic Byway**. It has been recognized by numerous travel publications and websites as one of the most beautiful drives in the country. The journey is 68 miles and offers views of the Teton Range, as well as rolling farmland, historic towns, and abundant wildlife.

Additional hikes include:

- Table Mountain Trail, 11 miles, difficult
- Upper Palisades Lake Trail, 8 miles, moderate
- Teton Crest Trail, 40 miles, difficult
- Ice Cave Trail, 1.6 miles, easy

Recreational Sites
City of Rocks National Reserve

This unique geological site has granite monoliths that tower up to 60 stories tall. The reserve spans over 14,407 acres and offers climbers the unique opportunity to ascend these granite giants. Other ways to explore the area include biking, hiking, and horseback riding. In the winter, snowshoeing and skiing are popular.

Bruneau Dunes State Park

The tallest freestanding sand dunes in North America, with the highest reaching 470 feet, may be found in Bruneau Dunes State Park. Rent a sandboard and surf the sand waves, hike the nearby trails, or climb the dunes. The park also offers camping, bluegill, and bass fishing in the lakes, and stargazing at the park's public observatory.

Bruneau Dunes State Park, Idaho

My friend Josh visited the Bruneau Dunes State Park last summer and, on the spur of the moment, decided to rent a sandboard. Now, Josh is a fitness fanatic and a very competent surfer. After renting the board, one of the park rangers gave him a few pointers on sandboarding, but Josh decided he knew better. So instead of sitting on the board, he reckoned it should be easier to surf down a dune than face a rolling wave. You guessed it, he climbed to the top of a tall dune and attempted to sandboard standing up. All was well for the first few meters, but then Josh discovered that the ride on sand is not as smooth as on water, and he went tumbling head-over-heels down the dune. He remembers getting to the bottom and being glad to be alive until he saw a crowd of people watching. As he stood up, his face red, they cheered, and Josh waved, laughed, and walked away, enjoying his 15 minutes of fame.

Other recreation sites you may want to visit include:

- Craters of the Moon National Monument
- Bear Lake State Park
- Thousand Springs State Park
- Curlew National Grassland
- Adelmann Mine
- Hagerman Fossil Beds National Monument

Water Recreation

Lakes

The 5,330-acre **Payette Lake** is located in the Idaho highlands at a height of roughly 5,000 feet. The lake is in Ponderosa State Park, which has over 1000 acres of natural wilderness, camping areas, hiking paths, and unspoiled beauty on the peninsula extending out into the middle of Payette Lake.

Bear Lake straddles the Idaho-Utah borders and is called the "Caribbean of the Rockies" due to its impressive turquoise waters. This is caused by the lake's white limestone floor. An interesting fact about Bear Lake is that its waters house a fish called the Bonneville Cisco, a rare species that is only found in a few lakes in the world.

🔭 *Grayson and Rylee stood at the edge of a cliff on Bear Lake. Their hearts were racing with excitement. They couldn't help but notice a group of tourists nearby staring at them in confusion. They were wearing ridiculous outfits consisting of bright green jumpsuits and helmets covered with flashing lights. They grinned at each other and yelled out, "Who's ready for an adventure?!" The tourists looked at them skeptically, but they did not care. As they prepared to take the plunge, Grayson realized they had forgotten one crucial item: their parachutes. Rylee shrugged it off and jumped followed by Grayson, hoping for the best. The tourists watched in disbelief as they plummeted toward the water below, but to their surprise, they emerged unscathed, grinning from ear to ear. The tourists shook their heads in disbelief and muttered something about crazy Americans as Grayson and Rylee sauntered off, already planning their next adventure.*

More lakes in the area:

- Redfish Lake
- Alturas Lake
- Stanley Lake
- Lake Walcott

- Lake Cascade
- Magic Reservoir

Waterfalls

Shoshone Falls, Idaho

Shoshone Falls has a height of 212 feet and a width of 900 feet. These falls are higher than Niagara Falls and just as spectacular. During the peak flow season, the falls can reach a width of over 100 feet and the thundering sound of the water can be heard from miles away.

If you want fabulous views of the Snake River, take a visit to the **Perrine Coulee Falls**. The waterfall drops about 200 feet into a canyon that offers an astonishing view of the surrounding landscape. The falls are created by the Perrine Coulee Creek, which flows into the canyon and drops over a series of ledges before cascading into the pool below.

Other falls in the vicinity include:

- Salmon Falls

133

- Goose Creek Falls
- Bear Creek Falls

Hot Springs

Boat Box Hot Springs is a unique hot spring that is very exclusive. The reason for this is that the "hot springs" are a metal tub on the banks of Salmon River in the Sawtooth National Forest about four miles from Stanley. The hot springs are a favorite destination for hikers, campers, and kayakers. The springs are made up of several natural pools, each with a different temperature and size, providing guests the opportunity to relax and soak in the warm water encircled by rocky cliffs, trees, and the flowing Salmon River, making it a picturesque and serene setting.

After their kayaking trip to the Boat Box Hot Springs, Rob and Sarah couldn't resist hopping into the metal tub. The warm water was sedative, and they felt the tension in their muscles melting away from their bodies. Suddenly, a bird flew overhead and landed on Rob's head. He jumped up in surprise, causing the tub to rock just a bit. Sarah's laughter filled the air as they tried to steady themselves and the tub. As Rob sat back down, they couldn't help but wonder what other unexpected visitors might come by for a soak. They sat in the tub, feeling both relaxed and on alert for the next few hours with grins on their faces.

Charles Kirkham discovered the **Kirkham Hot Springs** in the late 1800's while searching for gold in the area. The pools are arranged in a series of cascading terraces, with the hottest water at the top and the cooler water flowing down to the lower pools. This natural arrangement allows guests to choose the temperature that suits them best.

Boat Box Hot Springs, Idaho

Other hot springs you may want to visit include:

- McCall Commercial Hot Springs
- Goldbug Hot Springs
- Sunbeam Hot Springs
- Bonneville and Pine Flats Hot Springs
- Rocky Canyon Hot Springs
- Mountain Village Hot Springs
- Frenchman's Bend Hot Springs
- Loftus Hot Springs

End Book Review Page

Share your journey

….through a travel guide to the Pacific Northwest. Your opportunity to tell others about a perfect resource for adventure, great cuisine, entertainment, and rejuvenation.

Imagine the cherished memories you'll help to create, strengthening bonds and fostering togetherness. Guide fellow travelers towards life changing opportunities by offering a review that can shape perspectives and allow others to enjoy the enriching benefits of travel.

Offer a review by scanning the QR code below or go to: bit.ly/43ypGb3

Thank you for taking the time to leave your simple review, as YOUR review makes a difference.

Let's continue to share the gift of travel.

Conclusion

We've been all over the Pacific Northwest, from Washington to Oregon and Idaho, through big cities and small towns, and we've seen how many things there are to do in the Pacific Northwest area.

This travel guide is meant to be your companion on your travels through the Pacific Northwest. It will be an invaluable resource that will save you time and money as it provides information about the best places to visit, recreational opportunities, restaurants not to be missed, along with loads of helpful tips. It will help you plan your trip better and to determine the best way to spend your money by helping you avoid making mistakes and finding out about things you didn't expect.

As a seasoned traveler who has spent many years in the area, the author gives you helpful information about local culture and customs and tells you about new and interesting things to do. Overall, investing in this practical travel guide will help you make the most of your trip, lead you to beautiful destinations, and suggest exciting activities. Are you ready to travel to the Pacific Northwest?

When you visit the Pacific Northwest, you will discover a place with natural beauty, cultural diversity, and adventure that can't be found anywhere else. With its tall mountains, lush forests, clear lakes and rivers, the area has a lot to offer outdoor enthusiasts, whether they want to get their hearts racing or just take a quiet walk-in nature.

One of the most popular outdoor activities in the region is hiking. With its diverse landscape, there are trails to suit all levels of ability and interest. In the Cascade Range, you can go mountaineering or rock climbing if you want a more strenuous adventure. Fishing is another popular activity. Anglers come from all over the world to fish for salmon and steelhead runs. The area also has a lot of rivers and lakes that are great for kayaking and rafting.

For those seeking a more urban experience, the Pacific Northwest has plenty to offer. The cities of Seattle, Portland, and Boise are among the most livable and exciting cities in North America. They feature a wealth of shopping, dining, and entertainment options. From the iconic Pike Place Market in Seattle to the thriving food scene in Portland and the abundance of outdoor activities of Boise, there is something for everyone in the area. The Pacific Northwest is also a cultural haven. Cities have thriving art, music, food, and drink scenes. The region's rich history and indigenous culture are evident in the many museums, galleries, and cultural events that take place throughout the year.

The diverse cuisines in the region all have one thing in common: the use of fresh, locally produced ingredients. From seafood to free-range cattle, a wide range of vegetables, berries, even mushrooms are proudly produced and used in commercial kitchens as well as in homes. Seafood is a big part of the cuisine in the Pacific Northwest. Salmon, halibut, crab, and clam chowder are all popular dishes that contain seafood. The region is also known for its wild game, such as elk and venison, which are often served as stews, roasts, or in hearty sandwiches. Aside from using fresh, local ingredients, the food in this area also uses flavors and cooking methods from Native American, Asian, and Mexican cultures, as well as from Europe and the Middle East.

Whether you enjoy a rustic camping experience or a luxury holiday home, solitude, or crowds, you will find it all in the Pacific Northwest. From the rugged beauty of the Cascade Range to the vibrant culture of the cities, this region has it all. Why not pack your bags and start exploring the Pacific Northwest today?

In short, the Pacific Northwest is a region that is truly like no other. With its stunning natural beauty, rich cultural heritage, and flourishing cities, it is a place that should not be missed. So, whether you are looking for an outdoor adventure, a cultural experience, or just a chance to relax and recharge, the Pacific Northwest is the perfect destination for your next trip!

Your feedback is important to us and would be greatly appreciated! If you have a moment, we would be grateful if you could share your thoughts on the book by leaving a review on Amazon.

We hope you had a great experience reading the book and that it has inspired you to explore the Pacific Northwest.

References

- Airbnb. (2023). Skagit Valley Farmland View Cabin - Guesthouses for Rent in Mount Vernon, Washington, United States. Airbnb. https://www.airbnb.co.za/rooms/29011296?source_impression_id=p3_1670813629_cVvcxXqR%2BgX3kYxx&locale=en&_set_bev_on_new_domain=1673605396_MGRmNjZmZDk5YzI1

- Alderbrook Resort and Spa. (2023). Restaurants in Union WA - The Restaurant at Alderbrook Resort. Alderbrook Resort and Spa. https://www.alderbrookresort.com/culinary/restaurant

- Alex. (2022, August 11). Pacific Northwest Travel Guide. Audley Travel. https://www.audleytravel.com/usa/country-guides/pacific-northwest#:~:text=Best%20time%20to%20visit%20the

- Ambrose, W. V. (2008). Teacher's Guide For Pacific Northwest. https://dcmp.org/guides/TID7638.pdf

- Area Information | Olympic National Park & Forest | Olympic Peninsula WA. (n.d.). Olympic. Retrieved January 3, 2023, from https://www.olympicnationalparks.com/discover/area-information

- Ashbaugh, J. G. (2020, January 24). Pacific mountain system | mountains, North America. Encyclopedia Britannica. https://www.britannica.com/place/Pacific-mountain-system

- Banks, E. (2022, July 19). 6 Reasons to Drive to Port Townsend, Washington. Thrillist. https://www.thrillist.com/travel/seattle/things-to-do-port-townsend-washington

- Barros, P. (2012, March 3). Carrie Brownstein: the Northwest's funny girl. The Seattle Times. https://www.seattletimes.com/pacific-nw-magazine/carrie-brownstein-the-northwests-funny-girl

- Bay, S., & 2022. (2022, October 22). Seattle Is the Ultimate City for Outdoor Adventure Lovers — Here's How to Make the Most of It. Travel + Leisure. https://www.travelandleisure.com/trip-ideas/nature-travel/seattle-outdoor-attractions

- Blitz, M. (2015, August 4). Visit the World's Most Amazing Old-Growth Forests. Smithsonian; Smithsonian.com. https://www.smithsonianmag.com/travel/amazing-old-growth-forests-world-180956083

- Booker, C. (2022, May 14). Seattle Packing List (25 Things You Might Forget to Bring) - Travel Lemming. Travellemming.com. https://travellemming.com/seattle-packing-list

- Bossick, K. (2023). Coeur D'Alene: Idaho's "Little Slice of Heaven." Visit the USA. https://www.visittheusa.com/experience/coeur-dalene-idahos-little-slice-heaven

- Briney, A. (2019, July 23). Learn 10 Important Geographic Facts About the Pacific Northwest. ThoughtCo. https://www.thoughtco.com/ten-facts-about-the-pacific-northwest-1435740#:~:text=The%20Pacific%20Northwest%20is%20the

- Brown, A. (2020, June 23). Epic Road Trip Ideas for Washington State. TripSavvy. https://www.tripsavvy.com/great-washington-state-road-trips-4040149

- Buchan, E. (2020, June 16). Meet the famous fish throwers of Seattle's Pike Place Market. National Geographic. https://www.nationalgeographic.co.uk/travel/2020/06/meet-the-famous-fish-throwers-of-seattles-pike-place-market

- Burns, A. (2022, December 31). Idaho Scenic Train Rides: A Complete Guide (2023). American-Rails.com. https://www.american-rails.com/id-trdes.html

- Campuzano, E. (2018, February 2). k.d. lang would love nothing more than to hit the studio with

Damian Lillard. Oregonlive. https://www.oregonlive.com/music/2018/02/kd_lang_would_love_to_collaborate_with_damian_lillard.html

- Castillo, A. (2021, March 5). Top 30 Bible Verses About Nature And Its Beauty. Christian.net. https://christian.net/resources/top-30-bible-verses-about-nature-and-its-beauty
- Chateau Ste. Michelle. (2023). Woodinville Wine Tasting & Winery Tours | Chateau Ste. Michelle. Www.ste-Michelle.com. https://www.ste-michelle.com/visit-us/chateau-experience
- City of Seattle. (2023). Seattle Center. Www.seattlecenter.com. http://www.seattlecenter.com
- Citybob. (2023). 10 BEST Things to do at Washington State History Museum. Citybop. https://citybop.com/wa/washington-state-history-museum
- Clement, B. J. (2015a). What is Pacific Northwest cuisine? The Seattle Times. https://projects.seattletimes.com/2015/what-is-pacific-northwest-cuisine
- Clement, B. J. (2015b, November 11). On Vashon, Matt Dillon's happy pigs, vocal sheep and food philosophy. The Seattle Times. https://www.seattletimes.com/life/food-drink/on-vashon-matt-dillons-happy-pigs-vocal-sheep-and-food-philosophy
- Codeth. (2022, April 23). What to Pack for Your Trip to the Oregon Coast – Wander Blog. Wander. https://www.wander.com/article/what-to-pack-for-your-trip-to-the-oregon-coast
- Corbett, P. (2021, January 25). Top 10 True Western Towns of 2021. True West Magazine. https://truewestmagazine.com/article/top-10-true-western-towns-of-2021
- Dermody, K. C. (2022a, April 26). 9 Outdoor Adventures To Put On Your Pacific Northwest Bucket List. Trips to Discover. https://www.tripstodiscover.com/outdoor-adventures-in-the-pacific-northwest
- Dermody, K. C. (2022b, August 27). 23 of the Pacific Northwest's Best Destinations - TripsToDiscover. Trips to Discover. https://www.tripstodiscover.com/23-of-the-pacific-northwests-best-destinations
- Editors of Encyclopedia Britannica. (2023a). Spokane River | river, United States | Britannica. Www.britannica.com. https://www.britannica.com/place/Spokane-River
- Editors of Encyclopedia Britannica. (2023b). Wenatchee | Washington, United States | Britannica. Www.britannica.com. https://www.britannica.com/place/Wenatchee-Washington
- Editors of Encyclopedia Britannica. (2023c, January 2). Sarah Palin | Biography & Facts. Encyclopedia Britannica. https://www.britannica.com/biography/Sarah-Heath-Palin
- Eidtors of Encyclopedia Britannica. (2019). Idaho | History, Economy, People, & Facts | Britannica. In Encyclopædia Britannica. https://www.britannica.com/place/Idaho
- Expedia. (2023). Visit La Conner: 2023 Travel Guide for La Conner, Washington | Expedia. Expedia.com. https://www.expedia.com/La-Conner.dx55780
- Fralic, B. (2022, July 20). Tackling Twin Lakes Road in the North Cascades. Bellingham.org. https://www.bellingham.org/articles/tackling-twin-lakes-road-in-the-north-cascades
- Franklin House. (n.d.). ABOUT US. Franklin House. Retrieved January 5, 2023, from https://www.franklinhouseboise.com/about-us
- Fremch-American Chamber of Commerce. (2023, January 2). The Pacific Northwest. FACC Pacific Northwest. https://www.faccpnw.org/about-us/the-pacific-northwest.html
- Frisk, H. (2015). Columbia River Gorge. The Seven Wonders of Washington State. http://www.sevenwondersofwashingtonstate.com/the-columbia-river-gorge.html
- FRS Clipper. (2018, March 1). Newest High-Speed Victoria Clipper Ferry to Start Service on March 9. Clipper Vacations. https://www.clippervacations.com/media-

releases/newest-high-speed-victoria-clipper-ferry-start-service-march-9

- Garvin, E. (2019, August 19). Sand, Seafood and Surf in Coos Bay. Travel Oregon. https://traveloregon.com/things-to-do/outdoor-recreation/sand-seafood-and-surf-in-coos-bay

- Grambush, J. (2017, October 31). 15 Reasons Why You Should Visit Washington State. Culture Trip. https://theculturetrip.com/north-america/usa/washington/articles/15-reasons-why-you-should-visit-washington-state

- Grand Coulee Chamber of Commerce. (2023). Home. Grand Coulee Dam. https://grandcouleedam.org/

- gretatravels. (2017, May 8). BEST TRAVEL QUOTES: 55 Most Inspirational Travel Quotes Of All Time. Greta's Travels. https://gretastravels.com/20-best-travel-quotes

- Hartness, S. (2022, November 17). 50 Interesting & Fun Facts About Idaho State You Should Know. Destguides. https://www.destguides.com/united-states/idaho/idaho-facts

- Hiking Project. (2023). Hiking Trails near Northeast Washington. Hiking Project. https://www.hikingproject.com/directory/8010905/northeast-washington

- Huckleberry Press. (2019, April 21). Waterfalls of Northeast Washington. Huckleberry Press. https://huckleberrypress.com/waterfalls-of-northeast-washington

- Idaho State Historical Society. (2023). Old Idaho Penitentiary. Idaho State Historical Society. https://history.idaho.gov/oldpen

- Idaho State Parks and Recreation. (2023, January 9). Registration & Permits. Department of Parks and Recreation. https://parksandrecreation.idaho.gov/registration-permits

- Idaho, A. (2023). Farragut State Park. Department of Parks and Recreation. https://parksandrecreation.idaho.gov/parks/farragut

- Jahn, E. (2021, May 12). The far-out, spacey land sailors of Oregon's Alvord Desert. Opb. https://www.opb.org/article/2021/05/12/the-far-out-land-sailors-of-oregons-alvord-desert

- Jordan, A. (2017, June 16). 6 Reasons Why You Need to Visit Oregon. Culture Trip. https://theculturetrip.com/north-america/usa/oregon/articles/6-reasons-why-you-need-to-visit-oregon

- La Conner Chamber of Commerce. (2022). Romantic Getaways Washington State - La Conner on Top! Lovelaconner.com. https://lovelaconner.com/romantic-getaways-washington-state

- Lake Chelan Chamber of Commerce. (2023). Four Seasons of Sun and Adventure in Lake Chelan. Lake Chelan Chamber of Commerce. https://www.lakechelan.com/seasons

- Lane, B. (2019). 11 Top-Rated Campgrounds at North Cascades National Park | PlanetWare. Planetware.com. https://www.planetware.com/washington/top-rated-campgrounds-at-north-cascades-national-park-us-wa-149.htm

- Lane, B. (2020a, March 10). 12 Best State & National Parks in Washington | PlanetWare. Www.planetware.com. https://www.planetware.com/washington/best-state-national-parks-in-washington-us-wa-84.htm

- Lane, B. (2020b, December 11). 13 Best Beaches in Washington State. Www.planetware.com. https://www.planetware.com/washington/best-beaches-in-washington-state-us-wa-163.htm

- Lane, B. (2022, October 14). 10 Best Cities in Oregon | PlanetWare. Www.planetware.com. https://www.planetware.com/oregon/best-cities-in-oregon-us-or-93.htm

- Mandagie, B., & Mandagie, E. (2022, June 4). 34 Impressive and Fun Facts About Washington State - The Mandagies. Www.themandagies.com. https://www.themandagies.com/fun-facts-about-washington-state

- Mann, D. (2020, August 18). New Discovery show stars Jim Belushi's Rogue River pot grow. Mailtribune.com. https://mailtribune.com/top-stories/2020/08/18/new-discovery-show-stars-jim-belushis-rogue-river-pot-grow

- Marcus, G. (2001, July 9). https://time.com/section/articles/. Time. https://time.com/time/subscriber/article/0

- McKee, S. (2023, January 4). 15 Restaurants in Idaho That Will Blow Your Tastebuds Out Of Your Mouth. Movoto Real Estate. https://www.movoto.com/guide/id/idaho-restaurants

- McMenamins Pub. (2023). Elks Temple - McMenamins Pub at Elks Temple - McMenamins. Www.mcmenamins.com. https://www.mcmenamins.com/elks-temple/mcmenamins-pub-at-elks-temple

- Meis, S. (2022, January 3). 35 Things to Do in the Pacific Northwest 2023 | Clipper Vacations. Clipper Vacations Magazine. https://www.clippervacations.com/magazine/pacific-northwest-trip-ideas

- Metroparks Tacoma. (2023). Zoo Experience. Point Defiance Zoo & Aquarium. https://www.pdza.org

- Misachi, J. (2019, May 21). Which States Are In The Pacific Northwest? WorldAtlas. https://www.worldatlas.com/articles/which-states-are-in-the-pacific-northwest.html

- Mittge, B. (2015, June 12). The Daily Chronicle | The Daily Chronicle. Www.chronline.com.

- https://www.chronline.com

- National Geographic. (2011, August 9). Idaho Falls, Idaho, America's Best Adventure Towns -- National Geographic. Adventure. https://www.nationalgeographic.com/adventure/article/idaho-falls-idaho

- National Park Service. (2016). Weather - Olympic National Park (U.S. National Park Service). Nps.gov.

- https://www.nps.gov/olym/planyourvisit/weather.htm

- Newberry, K. (2011, August 18). For the Love of Cheese. Travel Oregon. https://traveloregon.com/things-to-do/eat-drink/culinary-experiences/for-the-love-of-cheese

- Northwest Maritime Center. (2023). Wooden Boat Festival. Port Townsend Wooden Boat Festival. https://woodenboat.org

- Northwest Trek Wildlife Park. (2023). Park Experience. Northwest Trek. https://www.nwtrek.org/visit/open

- Official Seattle Mariners Website MLB. (2019). Official Seattle Mariners Website. MLB.com.

- https://www.mlb.com/mariners

- Ohlson, B. (2022, August 2). When to visit Washington State to enjoy the best of the Pacific Northwest. Lonely Planet. https://www.lonelyplanet.com/articles/best-time-to-visit-washington-state

- Olympic Peninsula Tourism Commission. (2022). Visit Port Townsend | Things To Do | The Olympic Peninsula, WA. Olympic Peninsula. https://olympicpeninsula.org/destinations/port-townsend

- Oregon Coast Visitors Association. (2023a). South Beach State Park. Oregon Coast Visitors Association. https://visittheoregoncoast.com/cities/south-beach/activities/south-beach-state-park

- Oregon Coast Visitors Association. (2023b). Tillamook. Oregon Coast Visitors Association.

- https://visittheoregoncoast.com/cities/tillamook

- Oregon Parks Forever. (2023, January 9). Park Passes. Oregon Parks Forever. https://www.orparksforever.org/parking-passes

- Oregon State Parks. (2023). Tumalo State Park - Oregon State Parks. Stateparks.oregon.gov. https://stateparks.oregon.gov/index.cfm?do=park.profile&parkId=34

- Ossello, E. (2016, June 10). Washington's 80 Best Day Hikes. Outdoor Project. https://www.outdoorproject.com/travel/washingtons-80-best-day-hikes

- Pajama Jack. (2023). 6 Best Beaches in the Pacific Northwest. Panama Jack®. https://panamajack.com/blogs/at-the-beach/6-best-beaches-in-the-pacific-northwest

- Peterson, D. (2017, June 30). The Undiscovered Blue Mountains of Washington and Oregon.

Northwest Travel Magazine. https://nwtravelmag.com/undiscovered-blue-mountains-washington-oregon

- Reed, C. (2022, March 9). The NW Film Center Changes Its Name to PAM CUT. What Does That Mean? Portland Monthly. https://www.pdxmonthly.com/arts-and-culture/2022/03/nw-film-center-rename-pam-cut
- Richard, M. (2022, October 14). You might be surprised to learn that U.S. citizens can technically travel domestically without any ID at all. The Manual. https://www.themanual.com/travel/do-you-need-a-passport-to-travel-in-the-us
- Schmit, J. (2022, May 29). The 11 Best Mt. Rainier Hikes to Add to Your Washington Bucket List. Uprooted Traveler.
- https://uprootedtraveler.com/mt-rainier-hikes
- Schnee, A. (2022, September 22). The Ultimate Guide to the Kaniksu National Forest. Alex on the Map.
- https://alexonthemap.com/kaniksu-national-forest
- Schotland, M. J. (2015, July 21). Road Trip Bliss: Portland, Oregon to Boise, Idaho. Urban Bliss Life.
- https://urbanblisslife.com/portland-oregon-to-boise-idaho
- Seattle Art Museum. (2023). Seattle Art Museum. Www.seattleartmuseum.org. https://www.seattleartmuseum.org/visit/seattle-art-museum
- Spokane Visitor Information Center. (2017). Visit Spokane Washington | Things to Do, Hotels & Events. Visitspokane.com.
- https://www.visitspokane.com
- Staff, E. (2018, April 10). 38 Essential Restaurants in Seattle, Fall 2021. Eater Seattle. https://seattle.eater.com/maps/best-restaurants-seattle-38
- State of Idaho. (2023, January 6). Travel. Idaho Transportation Department. https://itd.idaho.gov/travel
- Sue, E. (2019, April 13). 5 Reasons Why the Pacific Northwest Should be on Your Bucket List • Explorer Sue. Explorersue.com. https://www.explorersue.com/pacific-northwest-bucket-list
- The Amplified Bible. (2023). Psalm 8:3 AMP - - Bible Gateway. Www.biblegateway.com. https://www.biblegateway.com/passage/?search=Psalm+8%3A3&version=AMP
- The Editors of Encyclopedia Britannica. (2018, February 19). Blue Mountains | mountains, Oregon-Washington, United States. Encyclopedia Britannica. https://www.britannica.com/place/Blue-Mountains-Oregon-Washington
- The Editors of Encyclopedia Britannica. (2019). Northwest | Description, States, & Facts. In Encyclopædia Britannica. https://www.britannica.com/place/Northwest-region
- The Oregon Coast. (2023). Cannon Beach. Oregon Coast Visitors Association. https://visittheoregoncoast.com/cities/cannon-beach
- The Pacific Science Centre. (2023). About PacSci. Pacific Science Center. https://pacificsciencecenter.org/about
- The Wilder. (2023). The Wylder | Craft Pizza & Cocktails | Boise. The Wylder Boise. https://www.thewylderboise.com
- Touropia. (2022, December 28). 12 Best Cities in Idaho to Live and Visit. Touropia. https://www.touropia.com/best-cities-in-idaho-to-live-and-visit
- Travel Oregon. (2017). Travel Oregon. Travel Oregon. https://traveloregon.com/places-to-go/regions/columbia-river-gorge/
- Travel Oregon. (2023a). Heceta Head Lighthouse. Travel Oregon. https://traveloregon.com/things-to-do/culture-history/lighthouses/heceta-head-lighthouse
- Travel Oregon. (2023b). Portland, OR: Find the BEST of Portland Travel & Tourism. Travel Oregon.
- https://traveloregon.com/places-to-go/cities/portland
- TravelOceanShores. (2022). Festival of Colors - Travel Ocean Shores %. Travel Ocean Shores.

- http://traveloceanshores.com/event/festival-of-colors
- Tri Cities Washington. (2023). Tri Cities Washington - Kennewick - Pasco - West Richland. Visit Tri-Cities.
- https://www.visittri-cities.com
- Tripadvisor. (2023a). BANANA LEAF THAI BISTRO, Port Townsend - Menu, Prices & Restaurant Reviews. Tripadvisor. https://www.tripadvisor.com/Restaurant_Review-g58687-d1504579-Reviews-Banana_Leaf_Thai_Bistro-Port_Townsend_Washington
- Tripadvisor. (2023b). Pizzeria Credo, Seattle - West Seattle - Menu, Prices & Restaurant Reviews. Tripadvisor. https://www.tripadvisor.co.za/Restaurant_Review-g60878-d4765938-Reviews-Pizzeria_Credo-Seattle_Washington.html#REVIEWS
- U.S. Department of Agriculture. (2014). Sawtooth National Forest - Sawtooth National Recreation Area. Usda.gov. https://www.fs.usda.gov/recarea/sawtooth/recarea/?recid=5842
- U.S. Department of Agriculture. (2023). Lolo National Forest - Home. Usda.gov. https://www.fs.usda.gov/lolo#:~:text=The%20Lolo%20National%20Forest%20is
- Underground Tour. (2015). UNDERGROUND TOUR. Www.undergroundtour.com. http://www.undergroundtour.com/
- United States Government. (2023, January 6). How to Enter the United States | USAGov. Www.usa.gov. https://www.usa.gov/enter-us#:~:text=All%20travelers%20entering%20the%20United
- United States Transportation Security Administration. (2019). Transportation Security Administration. Transportation Security Administration.
- https://www.tsa.gov
- University of Idaho. (2023). 9 Reasons to Fall in Love with Moscow. Www.uidaho.edu. https://www.uidaho.edu/admissions/admitted/things-to-know/love-moscow
- Wine and Jazz Festival. (2023). Vancouver Wine & Jazz Festival - Home. Vancouver Wine & Jazz Festival.
- https://www.vancouverwinejazz.com
- Visit Central Oregon. (2022). La Pine. Visit Central Oregon. https://visitcentraloregon.com/cities/la-pine
- Visit Idaho.org. (2023, January 6). Discover North Idaho. Visit North Idaho. https://visitnorthidaho.com
- Visit Oregon. (2022, May 1). Best Time To Visit Oregon | Visit Oregon. Visitoregon.com. https://www.visitoregon.com/best-time-to-visit-oregon
- Visit Seattle. (2023). Chateau Ste. Michelle Winery. Visit Seattle. https://visitseattle.org/partners/chateau-ste-michelle-winery-pd
- Visit Vancouver WA. (2023). 10 Reasons to Visit Vancouver, WA | Fun & Adventure. Www.visitvancouverwa.com. https://www.visitvancouverwa.com/trip-planning/10-reasons-to-visit
- VisitTheUSA. (2023). Pocatello. Visit the USA. https://www.visittheusa.com/destination/pocatello
- VRBO. (2023a). Renovated Log Cabin on Acreage, Sleeps up to 4 - Jefferson County. Vrbo.
- https://www.vrbo.com/579676
- VRBO. (2023b). Romantic Riverfront Cottage - 1 Mile to Winthrop! - Okanogan County. Vrbo. https://www.vrbo.com/4720028ha?noDates=true&unitId=5691411
- Vrbo. (2023a). Blue Starfish by AvantStay | Ocean Views & Direct Cannon Beach Access - Tolovana Park. Vrbo. https://www.vrbo.com/2565249?noDates=true&petIncluded=true&unitId=3135499
- Vrbo. (2023b). Handy Hangout - Long Beach. Vrbo. https://www.vrbo.com/1343613?noDates=true&unitId=1901961
- Vrbo. (2023c). NEW Listing - Little Elk Cabin ~ Hot Tub, Ski, Relax! - Packwood. Vrbo.

https://www.vrbo.com/3085664?noDates=true&unitId=3657722

- Walker, E. (2020, February 5). Falling in love with Sun Valley, the Idaho resort town where Hemingway lived and died. Roadtrippers. https://roadtrippers.com/magazine/hemingway-sun-valley-idaho/#:~:text=Hemingway%20was%20initially%20invited%20to

- Washington State Department of Transportation. (2023, January 8). Travel Washington Intercity Bus WSDOT.Wsdot.wa.gov. https://wsdot.wa.gov/business-wsdot/grants/public-transportation-grants/grant-programs-and-awards/travel-washington-intercity-bus

- Washington State Parks. (2023a). Deception Pass State Park | Washington State Parks and Recreation Commission. Www.parks.wa.gov. https://www.parks.wa.gov/497/Deception-Pass

- Washington State Parks. (2023b). Mount St. Helens Visitor Center | Washington State Parks and Recreation Commission. Www.parks.wa.gov. https://www.parks.wa.gov/245/Mount-St-Helens

- Washington State University. (2015). Washington State Tree Fruit Facts | Integrated Pest Management | Washington State University. Integrated Pest Management. https://ipm.wsu.edu/specialty-crops/tree-fruit/tree-fruit-facts/

- Washington Trails Association. (2023). Kendall Katwalk. Washington Trails Association.

- https://www.wta.org/go-hiking/hikes/kendall-katwalk

- Whitman, M. (n.d.). Cascade Range – The Pacific Ring Of Fire Volcanoes. Mountain IQ. Retrieved January 4, 2023, from https://www.mountainiq.co/north-america/cascade-range

- Wikipedia. (2021, September 1). Pacific Northwest. Wikipedia. https://en.wikipedia.org/wiki/Pacific_Northwest#:~:text=in%20the%20world

Image References

- Adam Blank. August 12,2021. Portland, Oregon. Unsplash https://unsplash.com/photos/Ff4BbI31Czg
- Afif Ramdhasuma. December 18, 2021. Snow-light-city landscape. Pexels https://www.pexels.com/photo/snow-light-city-landscape-11014281/
- Angel Ceballos. December 16, 2020. Pike Place Fish Market. Unsplash https://unsplash.com/photos/31Kn7ONM0g4
- Alden Skeie. June 6, 2016. Boise, United States. Unsplash https://unsplash.com/photos/cBx1EygM3BM
- Brigette Werner. July 27,2012. Sea Lions Cave Seals. Pixabay https://pixabay.com/photos/sea-lions-cave-seals-sea-lions-cave-52892/
- Dan Meyers. June 13,2019. Painted Hills, Oregon. Unsplash https://unsplash.com/photos/ioCjFTX-IYA
- Everett McIntire. August 21, 2018. Mount Rainier National Park. Unsplash https://unsplash.com/photos/htya7MsBSDM
- ID: 12019. December 25,2012. Mount Hood, Oregon. Pixabay https://pixabay.com/photos/mount-hood-oregon-volcano-72366/
- Intricate Explorer. November 22, 2020. Bruneau Sand Dunes. Unsplash https://unsplash.com/photos/EumQnT83Nuw
- James Wheeler. April 26, 2014. Tulip fields. Pexels https://www.pexels.com/photo/photo-of-field-of-yellow-and-red-tulips-1487010
- Jo Heubeck and Domi Pfenninger. September 5, 2022. Cannon Beach, Oregon. Unsplash https://unsplash.com/photos/VS_1KaZ2AJA
- ID: 1160162385. July 5, 2019. Kendall Katwalk Trail, Snoqualmie Pass, Washington. istock. https://www.istockphoto.com/photo/kendall-katwalk-trail-snoqualmie-pass-gm1160162385-317477074?clarity=false
- Mike Doherty. October 9 2020. Four Orca whales from the CA51 pod. Unsplash. https://unsplash.com/photos/iyVSCpOZUj0
- Modonnell. July 8, 2020. Idaho Wilderness. Pixabay https://pixabay.com/photos/wilderness-river-mountains-nature-5381117/
- Nathan Anderson. August 18, 2016. White lighthouse beside sea. Unsplash https://unsplash.com/photos/VMInXXYydp0
- Poyson. May 1, 2014. Seattle Mount Rainier Washington. Pixabay https://pixabay.com/photos/seattle-mount-rainier-335225/
- Ratapan Anantawat. July 3, 2019. Seafood. Unsplash. https://unsplash.com/photos/VltYKuJ0Mng
- Ryan Fish. May 21, 2019. Shoshone Falls in Twin Falls Idaho. Unsplash https://unsplash.com/photos/3pOLNVp1ZUA
- Varadh Jain. May 24, 2021. Crater Lake. Unsplash https://unsplash.com/(Wiggins)photos/J5B1NDtaH50
- William McAllister. February 8, 2008. Photo of man fishing. Pexels https://www.pexels.com/photo/photo-of-man-fishing-3793366/
- Zhifei Zhou. August 1, 2015. Kerry Park Seattle, Washington State. Unsplash https://unsplash.com/photos/QEob0Fp4rdg

Made in the USA
Las Vegas, NV
16 August 2023

76173069R00083